BECOMING PARENTS AND OVERCOMING OBSTACLES

BECOMING PARENTS AND OVERCOMING OBSTACLES
Understanding the Experience of Miscarriage, Premature Births, Infertility, and Postnatal Depression

Edited by
Emanuela Quagliata

KARNAC

First published in Italian in 2010 as *Diventare Genitori: Il concepimento, la gravidanza, il primo anno: la formazione di un legame profondo e le difficoltà del percorso* by Casa Editrice Astrolabio-Ubaldini Editore

First published in English in 2013 by
Karnac Books Ltd
118 Finchley Road
London NW3 5HT

British Library Cataloguing in Publication Data

A C.I.P. for this book is available from the British Library

ISBN-13: 978-1-78220-018-5

Typeset by V Publishing Solutions Pvt Ltd., Chennai, India

Printed in Great Britain

www.karnacbooks.com

CONTENTS

ABOUT THE EDITOR AND CONTRIBUTORS

Margaret Cohen trained as a child and adolescent psychotherapist and then as an adult psychotherapist at the Tavistock Clinic after reading philosophy at University College, London. She worked as a child psychotherapist at Great Ormond Street Hospital and then in a neonatal unit in a large inner-city hospital and also in paediatric oncology. She taught at the Tavistock Clinic and in Italy. She now has a private practice.

Hendrika C. Halberstadt-Freud is member of the International Psychoanalytic Association and the Association for Child Psychoanalysis. She is teacher, supervisor, and training analyst of two psychoanalytic societies in the Netherlands. She published *Electra vs Oedipus: The Drama of the Mother–Daughter Relationship* (Routledge, 2011), and *Men and Mothers: The Lifelong Struggle of Sons and Their Mothers* (Karnac, 2012), and many articles in journals in different languages. She worked in the child and adolescent psychiatry departments of the University of Amsterdam. Currently she is active in private practice.

Lisa Miller was for many years a consultant child psychotherapist in the child and family department at the Tavistock Clinic. Now partly retired, she continues to teach both in London and elsewhere. Although she considers herself to be a generalist with wide interests in all the different applications of child psychotherapy, Lisa Miller has had a particular interest in work with babies, small children, and their parents. For fifteen years she was the editor of the *International Journal of Infant Observation*, and the close observation of babies in the context of their families remains one of her leading preoccupations, not only for itself, but because of its relevance to clinical work.

Professor Joan Raphael-Leff, is both a psychoanalyst (Fellow, British Psycho-analytical Society; Member IPA) and social psychologist. She leads the UCL/Anna Freud Centre Academic Faculty for Psychoanalytic Research. Previously she was head of University College London's MSc in Psychoanalytic Developmental Psychology, and professor of psychoanalysis at the Centre for Psychoanalytic Studies, University of Essex. In 1998 she founded COWAP, the IPA's committee on Women & Psychoanalysis. For forty years she has specialised in reproductive and early parenting issues with over one hundred single-author publications, and eleven books in the field. She trains perinatal practitioners in many low- and high-income countries.

Marguerite Reid is a consultant child and adolescent psychotherapist who has worked in the field of perinatal mental health for many years. She co-founded the innovative perinatal service based at Chelsea and Westminster Hospital. She has carried out doctoral research in the area of perinatal loss and has subsequently specialised in clinical work where there has been a traumatic delivery. She has taught on the pre-clinical training at the Tavistock Clinic, London and on the Tavistock model course in both Rome and Venice. She co-founded an infant observation course in Izmir, Turkey and has taught in Istanbul. She has many publications in the area of perinatal mental health.

Emanuela Quagliata is a member of the Italian Psychoanalytic Society and of the International Psychoanalytic Association. She has carried out doctoratal research in the area of pregnancies at risk. She is a member of the Association of Child Psychotherapists (ACP, Tavistock Clinic), and teaches on the Tavistock- model course in psychoanalytical psychotherapy for infancy and adolescence in Rome and in Florence. She has taught at the Institute of Child Neuropsychiatry of the University of L'Aquila for ten years and worked in the foetal medicine unit of Rome hospital's gynaecological deptartment.

INTRODUCTION

There are many books that deal with pregnancy and maternity, and a large number of magazines and articles on paediatric nursing that examine these subjects from different points of view.

This volume is not a manual and is not intended to explain to future parents what to do and what to avoid. The objective is rather to look at the most significant and problematic aspects of this delicate phase of a woman's life and of that of a couple. It seeks to offer a key with which to understand the deep significance, and complexity, of the path to follow to become parents and to face fears linked to the difficulty of procreation, using the tools of observation and psychoanalytic listening.

Reviewing several experiences of clinical work, we offer our reflections on the personal experiences of women and couples and the difficulties which can be met when the desire for a child is disappointed. A maternity and parenting project can be frustrated by miscarriages and can encounter the fear of infertility. How are the problems of sterility or spontaneous abortion experienced? What are the consequences, on a psychological and emotional level, for parents and within the relationship with the child who is born after these painful experiences?

Children are born prematurely quite frequently and this is an event that can be a moment of intense suffering for parents. For many it is a deep trauma that they cannot "contain": anxiety over the survival of the child, feelings and fears, can find containment and be worked through within a therapeutic relationship.

After giving birth, a woman can experience a state of depression that conflicts with her joy of having brought a wanted child into the world. The birth of a child generally represents a moment of great joy for a woman and for the community that surrounds her. The birth, with its load of the unknown, of fears, fantasies, risks, and physical pain, is an event that now belongs to the past, like the difficulties and effort of pregnancy. It can even happen that a new mother does not feel as happy as perhaps she, more than anyone else, would have expected. Why does this happen? A chapter explores some situations that can predispose new mothers to post-natal depression.

Even if the traces of suffering cannot be cancelled, a painful experience can be faced and overcome if the person who has experienced it is helped to understand and work through it, with therapeutic intervention.

The authors deepen some problematic issues, describing ways of intervening, with the important preventive aim that the suffering of the parents should not compromise the emotional development of the child. The central idea of this work is that it is possible to get over a difficult beginning or relationship and that unresolved problems can be renegotiated at every stage of development. It is possible to recover from a moment of misunderstanding and disharmony within a couple and to promote the development of the relationship between mother and child. We have tried to show how the bond between them is formed in the absolute uniqueness of the relationship, facing the inevitable human limits which ensure that nothing is perfect.

This study is intended above all for parents, or future parents, but, naturally, also for psychologists, doctors, gynaecologists, obstetricians, and paediatricians, who can consider the complexity of these experiences from a new point of view.

Emanuela Quagliata

CHAPTER ONE

A paradoxical pain: recurrent miscarriage

Emanuela Quagliata

Despite a growing interest in matters regarding pregnancy and infertility, the impact of a woman's emotional response to the traumatic event of her previous miscarriages during a current pregnancy has received little research attention, although the broader category of stillbirth has been the subject of many studies. The existing literature has identified various emotional states associated with the interruption of pregnancy but seems to lack a deeper understanding of a meaningful connection between them.[1]

What particularly struck me was the degree of distress and the depth of loneliness that this event, so invisible from the outside but so traumatic and present inside, could elicit in the couples I met. As happens when a couple faces the news of the death of a baby that is already born, the moment of the negative ultrasound result represented the end of all the parents' unconscious fantasies about their unborn child and the collapse of all their plans, dreams, and hopes for the future of their child and their family: this reality was often faced in total isolation.

The depth and complexity of the pain and fear of another loss was often touchingly apparent in the couples, even if concealed behind very different individual behaviours and reactions. Talking to these women I became aware of how this experience, which I would call an "invisible loss", was accompanied by all the manifestations of mourning.

Listening to my patients' stories, the experience of their previous miscarriages was a subject which all of them felt the need to share from the first meeting. If, on the one hand, it seemed that they did manage to talk about it, even if only as part of the process of describing their current state, I think that a special urgency to do so originated from the pressing need to share a traumatic event which, in many cases, seemed not to have found a space to be understood at a deeper level; its unknown impact in their internal world may contribute to these women's difficulty in developing their identity. For almost all of them the first miscarriage was felt as particularly traumatic although they were told that these were things "that could happen", the sense of belonging to a large group did not helped to alleviate the impact of the event. A variable which turns out to be important in mitigating the traumatic effect of the loss of the baby was its predictability. By contrast, the second miscarriage was a relief for some mothers because they felt too ill, but for others the second miscarriage was not only unexpected, but also unexplained. What seemed to emerge from these experiences—which were different even in their similarity—was that it was not a question of how advanced the pregnancy might have been but that when the miscarriage followed a scan during which the baby's heartbeat had been heard, and after the first movements of the foetus had been felt, the event was accompanied by strong feelings of loss, anger, and shock. The contrast between life and death seemed to be more marked and violent in these cases: reality destroyed signs of life which had already been clearly experienced.

An interesting contribution shows how PTSD (post-traumatic stress disorder) is prevalent in pregnancies following stillbirth. Women were found to be vulnerable to PTSD in the pregnancy subsequent to stillbirth, particularly where conception occurs soon after the loss (Hughes, 2001). A pregnancy or a birth following a miscarriage are not necessarily helpful in processing the grief, and the complexity of the reaction to a loss of this nature cannot be simplistically resolved by a new conception (Lin & Lasker, 1996). In the light of many studies, in fact, it could be speculated that the emotional feelings stirred by death were avoided by conception thus inhibiting the mourning process by pregnancy (Lewis, 1979; Lewis & Casement, 1986).

What is certain, however, is that if the subsequent pregnancy results in a new loss, the intensity of grief experienced is increased to a comparable degree. All these feelings influence the new pregnancy and often do not help these mothers to enter into intimate contact with the vital and creative aspects associated with their new conception. In particular, the emotions experienced by the mother also profoundly affect the couple relationship. The previous failures, as well as the uncertainty surrounding the pregnancy and the risk of further miscarriage, are often the cause of tensions in such couples who are forced to live for many months in a state of doubt and uncertainty.

Every woman and every couple reacts in a unique and personal way to solitude and pain. But sometimes, in particular in the case of recurrent miscarriages, the trauma of this loss is so profound as to be not only difficult to work on and overcome, but can also compromise the stability of the couple, contaminate a subsequent pregnancy, and undermine a woman's own identity (see Raphael Leff, Chapter Five). Often the experience of the loss, and the need to cope with uncertainty, are factors associated with unconscious fantasies which render the experience deeply traumatic. The previous losses, and the threat of the loss of the baby during the new pregnancy, undermine the mother's trust in her creative capacities and raise persecutory feelings in relation to internal objects which are felt to distrust her capacity to become pregnant, to keep the pregnancy, and to give birth.

Unresolved earlier conflicts with the maternal figure are certainly intensified by the narcissistic wound received as a result of the devastating effect of the loss of these women's babies. Internal persecutory figures do not allow them to become mothers and fuel a conflict between the thoughts that encourage life and those that deal with death.

As well as the fear of another loss of a longed-for child, and the related unconscious fantasies, a further difficulty in confronting pregnancy and the possibility of another death of the foetus is the painful reawakening of feelings connected to the experience of unprocessed grief over previous deaths. This means that, if before or in conjunction with pregnancies, future parents have had to face important bereavement—such as, for example, the death of a parent—the thought of those deaths seems to return to life in the moment of a new conception and to influence the perception and fears about the new pregnancy. In this way, the 'unmetabolized' feelings are then reactivated at the time of the loss of the child and, also, the story of the new life seems to become inextricably entangled with the memories of the previous experiences of pain and death. It is important for these women to work through the loss of their previous pregnancies and to understand the significance that has been attributed to them.

Interesting hypotheses suggest that a relationship is created through chemical and biological messages between the mother and the foetus (Mancia, 1981), and also the observation of the foetus by ultrasound scanning (Piontelli, 1992), explore the subject of the balance between hereditary and environmental influences. Clinical experience has taken us increasingly further back, to trace how fundamental the very early stages of a child's life are for all of its future development: here we have arrived at the age of "minus three-quarters" (nine months before birth), in that area of pregnancy which is fundamental for preventive purposes.

Often the event of a spontaneous abortion tends to pass unnoticed, not only by the people who are emotionally closest to the woman undergoing the experience, but also by medical staff. Menzies Lyth, 1959) carried out an in-depth analysis of the defence mechanisms set in place by nursing and medical staff to protect themselves from the emotional pain and feelings about life and death which are intrinsically part of their work. It is not easy for medical staff to give special attention to women who present these ailments which interfere with their ability to procreate. The common experience was for women to encounter a tendency by staff to diminish the problem, as though it is no less difficult for them to face this "small", "invisible loss".

The memory of trauma and fear of a new start, the anxiety of being simultaneously in contact with life and death, the memory of a dead child and the identification with a precariously live one, are particularly unbearable. A painful event requires a great deal of working through in the mind: the ability to transform painful and undigested experiences into thoughts is what Bion referred to as "alpha function" (Bion, 1962). Ingham writes: "Trauma occurs when this work, alpha functioning, is overwhelmed and unable to contain and digest the quality and quantity of stimuli involved and therefore breaks down ... It is in the recognition and the acknowledgement of separateness and the working through of the experience of absence of the providing mother, that thought and mental work are constituted ... this process is essentially a mourning process" (Ingham, 1998, pp. 98–99).

Pregnancy is a time of psychological as well as physiological preparation and "a certain amount of anxiety in pregnancy, as in any other major life event, is an indication that this psychological work is taking place, that a woman is preparing herself by being receptive to the natural fears in the face of a situation which carries many unknown" (Breen, 1989, p. 7).

Women who have suffered previous miscarriages need to find a deep understanding of the unique nature of their experience. Psychoanalytically oriented interviews can help them to cope with the intense anxieties of a new pregnancy and can therefore play an important preventive role, as it is a way of protecting the development of the bond mothers will make with their new baby.

Anna: search of an identity and the sense of emptiness

"Pregnancy, particularly the first pregnancy, is a crisis point in the search for a female identity, for it is a point of no return, whether a baby is born at the end of term or whether the pregnancy ends in abortion or miscarriage" (Caplan, 1959; Pines, 1972). In particular, in the case of spontaneous abortion, this "crisis point" I think manifests itself in patients' experience as a trauma and as such represents "a breakdown of an established way of going about one's life, of established beliefs about the predictability of the world, of established mental structures, of an established defence organization" (Garland, 1998, p. 11).

Miscarriage can be experienced as an emotional earthquake which deeply undermines the confidence at the heart of women's identities and, therefore, their creative capacity. Naturally, the impact which a miscarriage has on a life can only be understood within the individual story which has given form to the individual's internal world. I found myself confronting differing levels of anxiety: there were women who, although they were going through similar experiences, had greater resources than others and different degrees of vulnerability. However, my impression was that, often, many of the women I met could not succeed in finding, in their internalreality, a maternal figure to help them gradually elaborate their pain and anxieties.

I was surprised to note that very often patients didn't want to get closer to their mothers at this difficult time except for the most practical support and I wondered what the role of the expectant mother's identification with her own mother might be during the course of the pregnancy. According to the psychoanalytical model, primary relationships influence the way in which events performed externally are constructed in the internal world. These early relationships inevitably influence the nature of the damage felt as loss, also determining the degree in which personal resources can cope with this damage.

Anna, aged thirty-two, was suffering from an autoimmune disease.[2] She came to the unit with a history of two miscarriages: the first, which occurred in the fifth month, terminated a pregnancy which had been full of problems from the start, sustained by means of therapies and bed rest and had happened about three months before our first meeting. The second miscarriage was in the fifth week of pregnancy and coincided exactly with the start of our sessions. The traumatic nature of the first miscarriage was the reason she had come to see the gynaecologist, Dr. V., and had then accepted the suggestion that she should come to see me.

Anna arrived for our first appointment with her husband. They both came from a town in the vicinity of Rome where both of their parents' families still lived, and had been married for four years. Although she could have been attractive, she tended to wear somewhat severe and outdated clothes which made her look older than her years. She was also very pale with dark shadows under her eyes which gave her an "ill" look and, without a trace of make-up, her eyes had a sad expression. I invited both of them to speak. He began to talk about the miscarriage which had occurred three months earlier, about the threats of miscarriage which his wife had from the start, the times she had been taken into accident and emergency, and the fact that, in spite of everything, the pregnancy had lasted up to the fifth month. She told me the exact date of the miscarriage and about the heart defect which had been diagnosed in the foetus. At the time she had been told: "In such cases nature takes care of itself", implying that in any event the child would have died shortly after its birth, but Anna kept on wondering why nature should have "taken care of itself" only at the fifth month, leaving things late enough for her to have seen her baby daughter sucking her thumb just the day before when she had had a scan. The pain attached to the loss of a baby at such an advanced stage of pregnancy is very intense, and I expressed my understanding to them. Following a pause which was heavy with sorrow, the husband forced a smile in an attempt to defuse the situation and added that his wife believed that she would also lose this child in spite of the fact that she was now being looked after by Dr. V, in whom she placed great trust. He emphasised Anna's "pessimistic nature" in contrast to him being an "optimist". In any case, the loss of the baby had also affected him greatly and had brought about a strong feeling of isolation in both of them. This was also due to the fact that the people with whom they had the closest friendships recently were four couples all of whom were expecting babies: the miscarriage had inevitably distanced them from the others who had had their children.

Anna told me of the great distress caused by her GP who, in the past, had merely given her some tranquillizers, whereas the gynaecologist advices her to see a psychotherapist. She also told me that she suffered from insomnia and that, for about three years, she had also been having panic attacks, which had been aggravated by the pregnancy. The onset of these attacks had coincided with the time of their move to Rome from a smaller town because of the husband's work: in the new city Anna had immediately felt even more isolated, unable of doing anything at all—even of driving the car or taking a bus—without being accompanied by someone. However, as far as the miscarriage was concerned, the night it came she was alone, but she was able to deal with it quite well despite the fact that her husband, who worked in public transport, was on night shift and she had thought she would never have been able to manage. Following the miscarriage they immediately tried to have another baby but it seemed reluctant to come, transforming every menstruation into a huge disappointment and increasing their anxiety. Finally conception occurred in October, much to Anna's surprise, given that, due to a psychological problem which she described as a "sense of emptiness", the couple had significantly reduced the frequency of their sexual relations.

As often happens, too little time was allowed to grieve for the first child and I observed how the past—the loss—seemed to invade the present. Anna remembered, with emotion, how she had heard her baby's heart-beat at the time of the last scan and now she feared that she would have to wait, once again, as long as the fifth month before knowing how it would all turn out. After all, she added, not even the doctors know, "only God knows!" A sad, tense moment followed this statement, which expressed all the gravity of the trauma experienced by the couple. Then the husband broke the silence pointing out, with surprise, how his wife was talking much more than she normally did. She confirmed that in general she felt uncomfortable with people and had done so ever since she had been a little girl. She told me that her father had been a teacher and that her class teacher had always been in competition with him: every time she made a mistake he would humiliate her publically in order to demonstrate that her father did not know how to teach. Unfortunately she had this same teacher for the whole five years of primary school. After this she always had problems with school but, notwithstanding these difficulties, she managed to do well in her final school exams. I observed that clearly she was capable of reacting and asserting herself in spite of her difficulties. But Anna responded saying that when things went well she considered it to be purely by chance whereas her husband was always cheerful and happy with things, even too much so.

Once again this difference emerged between them, further confirmed by a statement made by the husband regarding the fact that she was never affectionate and never gave him satisfaction. We explored her past experiences of finding herself interacting with people who made her feel discouraged and who devalued her, just as they used to when she was a child, and who, perhaps, continued to do so during her pregnancy; and she was reminded of her previous pregnancy, during which period she had been taken into hospital five times: every month she had suffered a haemorrhage. Then she recalled how, on the day of the miscarriage, there had been no room at the hospital, how her gynaecologist had not been there, and how she had not wanted to disturb him by calling him on the telephone. They had told her to push, but "it was hard to push knowing that afterwards it would all be over", she told me in a whisper. In the end she had done what they told her to do because there was no alternative. Still now, when she closed her eyes, she could see the same things she saw that day and could smell the smell of her pyjamas. Anna then asked me whether, in my view, she should have an amniocentesis test, but then immediately added that the risks of the test causing a miscarriage were not so very high: "Why should it have to be me who ends up in that nought point five per cent?" she concluded. I commented that this was a different way of seeing things, from a different perspective, but Anna reacted with surprise: it was the first time that anyone had drawn her attention to her ability to see things from a positive viewpoint.

At the end of the session, I thought that although it was really difficult to distance oneself from such painful memories, she seemed to feel more hopeful the moment she could find containment (Bion, 1962) for her pain. The traumatic memory of her previous experience still seemed to be very vivid and the anxiety and the urgency to immediately have another child, felt by other mothers, seemed to be a way of not dwelling on the past experience. The recollection of the memories of the earlier pregnancy transmitted this sense of loneliness to me, or rather, of pain experienced in solitude. I also found myself reflecting on the profound change that the move to a big city must have caused to this couple's life: she especially seemed to have lost her social recognition and, consequently, any clear sensation of having an identity. Moreover, I thought that the psychosomatic response was in the forefront and that the specific modality of the panic attacks were the means by which Anna's body registered her emotional reaction. During this first meeting there also emerged a deep and painful sense of lack of self-worth: the memory of the teacher, which was still strong, represented an evil internal object, repeating to her that she was not worth anything, that she would never make it. I thought that it was important to highlight her ability to react and to think in a constructive way. The very clear contrast between the husband's optimistic and confident attitude and that of his wife led me to wonder what effect this pronounced split might have on the couple at such an emotionally exhausting time in their relationship. Our journey together continued for two and a half years, starting at the time of her conception and carrying on to the birth of her son, and afterwards continuing with some brief observations of her life as a mother and her relationship with the child.

During work with Anna I was struck by the fact that she tended to delegate her ego function to me, for example, by asking me many questions during our meetings about how I perceived her and what I thought of her. For example, she asked me if I considered her to be a depressive or whether I thought she was lazy, if I thought she was normal or, more directly, what I thought of her. I think that having a high-risk pregnancy has a strong impact on women's identity and on their self-esteem. This would show itself in their inability to ignore the interference of other members of the extended family, especially mothers-in-law, by whom these expectant mothers felt oppressed and threatened. I think Anna made important progress in this regard, succeeding in defending her space with me and with the hospital, despite both of us having been harshly criticised and devalued by her family members. She said she "developed greater confidence". Having been able to attend sessions from the beginning of her pregnancy certainly helped to stem the deathly aspects and to reinforce her potential and vital resources.

Often the exchange between the couple bears witness to the difficulty and the suffering of having to go through a situation which is loaded with uncertainties and threats, as well as a particular self-perception as someone who, like Anna, does not feel worthy or up to the task. In the stories of many women, the relationship with their partner is character- ised by suffering and conflicts instead of being a source of possible sup- port. Many women, in fact, speaking of abortion, brought with them the experience of an earlier disappointment to do with the difficulty of communicating the physical experience of loss to others in general and to their own partner specifically: the many weeks of uncertainty and physical pain, the experience of the curettage, the difficulty in work- ing through the loss, and the forced immobility, were experiences the importance of which other people could not completely recognise, nor could they understand the individual and specific significance which the mother attributed to them.

From that dramatic impact, therefore, it seems that the impossibil- ity of communicating, deeply, their personal emotional and physical experience, brings couples to separate, not only in the sharing of emo- tional contents, but also in their attitudes and behaviours. Often the differences between partners in their ways of suffering risked causing a break-up of the relationship. A recurrent aspect was that related to a concrete marginalisation of the fathers, blocked off from their wives' ail- ments and from the pain shown by them, feeling passive and impotent. An example is given of feelings of exclusion, tension, and jealousy that can arise in a man when his wife refers to a male gynaecologist. In some cases this separation can also affect the area of sexuality, even arriv- ing at extreme situations: the husband is "left out", giving rise to what Bradley calls "a parthenogenic fantasy" (Bradley, 2000, p. 35) in which the baby is conceived without the man's involvement. In most couples, the husband was also a marginal or egocentric figure, and, especially, fearful of sharing feelings of distress associated with previous miscar- riages, and fugitive from his anxious wife. All this produced extraordi- nary pressure on women who had complications in pregnancy, as they felt these complications were threatening the source of identity: their own, their husband's, and that of the couple.

The experience of the two miscarriages had confirmed in Anna—as in other patients—pre-existing, unconscious fantasies about her inability to generate new life. There was no anger in her but rather the sensation of having a fixed destiny: she felt that she had death inside her and therefore feared that on the day of the dead she would produce a third dead baby. She seemed identified on the one hand with an internal object of death, which gave her the sensation of having to succumb to a pre-ordained destiny, whereas on the other, perhaps in an attempt to identify with her lost child, she felt empty and dead inside (Leon, 1990, p. 42).

Anna explained to me one day that the gynaecologist had discovered that her problem was due to a dysfunction in her immune system and that there was a "killer" (she is referring to the Natural Killer)[3] which was activated during her pregnancy: now the course of injections was inhibiting its action. I was struck by this information, which she told me rather unemotionally, and the description of her autoimmune problem in terms of this "killer" brought me back once again to her imaginings revolving around deathly and invasive forces present inside her body and now effectively "tracked down"; and also to the sensation of external invasive and deathly forces identified by Anna principally in the members of her husband's family and even in the husband himself.

Anna's intense anxiety derived from the perception of an internal enemy which, as we have already said, refuses women permission to become mothers; and at the same time this perception is confused with the "internal enemy" associated with the dysfunction of their immune systems, the "natural killer" which obstructs the proper development of their children. Therefore their own bodies are experienced, not as allies supporting the life of their babies and protecting them, but as external enemies who are not able to offer protection from the "killer". The presence of this mental and biological "internal enemy"—which, in Anna's case was not kept sufficiently at bay and was of a nature that could not easily be distanced from—generated intense persecutory feelings and fantasies of death.

From this point of view our work served to create space for the baby and to establish a female identity secure in the ability to create life. Anna felt more vital when she succeeded in establishing a positive maternal transference and in feeling in touch with a benign figure who believed in her ability to create life.

Claudia: pregnancy like an illness and a body that betrays

With regard to the theme of the relationship between mind and body, Irene Matthis's metaphor is particularly illuminating: lightning and thunder appear to the observer like two separate phenomena which are distant in time, whereas in reality they originate from a single physical phenomenon, a discharge of electricity (Matthis, 2000).

Listening to what women told me, I came to consider how the body influences the mind and vice versa. A woman's response to her symptoms is influenced by the symbolic meaning that she unconsciously attributes to her physical state. Raphael-Leff writes:

> There is, however, no simple psychosomatic connection [...]. The important factor is how these and other physical symptoms are emotionally interpreted by the woman. A troubled woman may experience her sickness as an attempt to rid herself of the parasitic invader by being violently ill; another feels she vomits because of being poisoned by the harmful foetus. An anxious woman may treat nausea as a sign of her internal insufficiency; a depressed one may feel it as her internal "badness" being disgorged. Some women welcome ongoing symptoms as a definite indication that they are still pregnant. (Raphael-Leff, 1993, p. 37)

In this sense, I noticed instead that, for these patients, who experience miscarriage, it was only at a certain stage, and with a degree of difficulty, that the movements of the foetus, the nausea, or other signals, could be interpreted as proof of the presence of a live baby. In fact the early months—but, in these particular cases, almost the entire pregnancy, at least until the foetus was past danger—seemed like time held in suspense, during which even the symptoms and their changes were not noticed.

Claudia was thirty-three and had been referred to the foetal medicine unit after having had two miscarriages the previous year, both of which occurred within the first twenty weeks of pregnancy.[4] She was now in the twenty-fourth week of a third pregnancy and feeling well, but she had suffered complications and had been forced to spend most of her pregnancy in bed. She had been married for two years. Before conceiving, Claudia had already been aware of the fact that a pregnancy would result in a deterioration of her condition and place her at risk of thrombosis. Claudia was a very pretty and cheerful woman, even though the steroid treatment had made her somewhat "round" and made her feel a bit "overweight". Her plump face, without make-up, was framed by dark hair which drew my attention to the brilliant blue colour and the intelligent look of her eyes. The actual diagnosis had only been made about six years after the first clinical symptoms (two years before she had come to the unit) and in the months immediately prior to the death of her mother. This was someone who was very important to Claudia, whom she often talked about during the sessions, and who had died of a pulmonary tumour which had been diagnosed too late; this was partly as a result of a certain negligence on the mother's own part in not going to check-ups and partly as a result of her lifestyle, which she had never changed, due to her disinclination to accept limits, in spite of all Claudia's efforts to persuade her to do so. Claudia had married three months after her mother's death, to keep a promise that she made to her to marry on the same date as her own wedding. Naturally, the preparations and the wedding itself were not a joyful experience. The joy of the pregnancy also seemed tinged with the sadness caused by the absence of her mother who, to cap it all, "had so longed for a little grandson", something Claudia felt she had failed to give her in time. During the course of the sessions, a father figure emerged with a difficult and selfish character who was jealous and resentful of the love which created the bond between the mother and her children and, in particular, with Claudia; and a couple of interfering parents-in-law who were anxious, anxiety-inducing, egocentric, vaguely hypochondriac, and decidedly incapable of defusing the situation and reassuring her. The disease made her pregnancies "different", both in reality and in her subjective experience: a higher risk of miscarriage, great concern for her own health and that of the baby, and fear of a potential hereditary problem.

From the outset of our sessions, the joy of her pregnancy was deeply interwoven with the distress over her own disease which had caused her to have two previous miscarriages, albeit in the very early stages of pregnancy. In particular, there was evidence of a perception of possible mutual damage which, in the case of the lupus, was not merely imaginary but rather more of a reality, given that pregnancy leads to an increase in antibodies, and the withholding of certain drugs leads to an increased risk of thrombosis. "At this time I am the one who is more at risk and so I am not calm".

Consequently, there was anxiety associated with the desire for a child and the fact of not being in good health. But, on the other hand, there was also fear over the consequences of the medication which she had to continue taking, and a doubt which was constantly present: what was she passing on to the baby? Therefore, from the first encounter, there were fundamentally three themes: distress over what was impossible to foresee; concern about what she might pass on to her daughter; but, above all, the idea that her daughter might have a mother who was ill.

The pregnancy, which had a fortnightly pattern established by a whole series of specific tests, was experienced like an illness. Claudia described being ill as being like "having to deal with an unknown force which is killing you!" This was mainly due to the impossibility of knowing the causes of lupus and to its asymptomatic nature. This latter feature of her illness led her to associate it with her mother's disease, a tumour on the lung, which had led to her death in the space of just a few months. Her grief over the loss of her mother continued to stand in the way of her joy over her pregnancy: "My mother not being here makes my pregnancy less joyful than that of my friends". And again: "There was no pleasure in going to choose the wedding dress and all the rest without her". This harrowing perception of her loss was now accompanied by a sense of guilt—because her mother would have so longed for a grandchild and, now that the time was approaching, she was not able to enjoy it—but, at the same time, it also brought with it the memory of the discussions she had had with her mother to persuade her to have a check-up with a doctor, which was something she had never done: "It was as though she had always known that there would be a bad problem and she did not want to see it".

The initial focus of our work was therefore the question of knowing and not knowing: how, unlike her own mother, Claudia could have important information about her illness, but also how to know/recognise her own feelings, including those of anger and resentment. And, in the specific instance, how our meetings could help her to modulate and contain the feelings of distress which arose from this knowledge. In this particular discussion, Claudia adopted an argumentative position with regard to the doctors, remembering her mother's illness, diagnosed too late, and her own previous gynaecologist, who had not made her take the right tests. Who was able to identify problems and what should be done once a problem had been identified? She told me about a doctor who had told her that she could go to a hot country for her honeymoon,

"when everyone knows that with lupus one can't go out in the sun!",
as Claudia said ironically. But then she went all the same! Even though
she was in dispute with the specialist who gave her the wrong advice,
she herself consciously made the wrong choice. A more general difficulty Claudia had in accepting limits began to emerge, demonstrated
initially by this inability to make a sacrifice. And it was always as part
of this substantial difficulty that Claudia tried to understand and justify
her mother's not wanting to see her own illness and the way she subsequently did nothing to help herself get better: "She had many problems
and she dealt with them by smoking; it was as though the cigarette was
the thing which kept her in equilibrium … until in the end she went to
her chemotherapy sessions smoking …" Gradually, her mother's problems were linked principally to the difficulty in the parents' relationship and this also brought to light the resentment Claudia felt towards
her father, who was now "playing the victim" and "had not reacted like
a father when I told him that I was pregnant" because "he wants all the
attention for himself". "I lost my mother but it's as though I had lost
both of my parents".

By exploring the subject of limits and impositions gradually, Claudia
reflected on the fact that, if, on the one hand, she could not tolerate impositions, it emerged that she would begin many things with
enthusiasm and then stop them without any apparent motive. She
began to feel that, perhaps, on some occasions, she might have been in
need of a firmer approach on her parents' part, such as, for example, in
the matter of her failure to complete her university course, which even
then remained a source of guilt for her. Thus the onset of the symptoms
of her illness was associated with the time when she dropped out of
university and did not know what to do with her future, and its full
presentation with the moment when she understood the seriousness
of her mother's illness: "Some say that autoimmune diseases have an
emotional basis … I am certain of it!" The exploration of these feelings,
and their connection with her illness, seemed to make Claudia feel that
there were important things which had been brought to light by her
pregnancy and she asked me "And what next?", wondering whether
there would be the possibility of continuing with the sessions after she
had had the baby, as if to ask: "Once the pregnancy is over, will you still
look after me?"

So, gradually, over the course of the sessions, the subject of "looking
after" became a constant theme.

In the sixth month Claudia felt that the period of greatest risk was over. She had to look after herself, as if to say: "The baby exists and I have to deal with it". In actual fact, looking after her mother had been driven primarily by the fear of losing her: "It must have been the panic at the prospect of losing my mother that made me discover this part of my character"; but her idea of how she had looked after her was not positive: "I don't know how to look after myself and the idea of looking after someone else frightens me, but they say it is a maternal instinct", she said, smiling. So in the end there was something good, an internal maternal figure upon whom she could lean and on whom she could rely—a maternal instinct.

Giulia was born in the thirty-fifth week by caesarean section. Claudia was well and her baby did not need to go into an incubator: she seemed to feel that her uterus had managed to do its job for long enough to spare her baby that experience and she felt this to be a strong point to her credit. Guilia was a lovely baby and Claudia was amused by her thick black hair. But above all she was surprised by her baby's ability to make herself understood so well: "Today she was hungry and she started to cry big tears, even the nurse was astonished!" This aspect of the baby seemed to be reassuring for this mother who had been so worried that she would not to be able to interpret the needs of her little one.

At this point in time Claudia, understandably, seemed to forget all her painful feelings, but, at the same time, she remained aware of the fact that she had some problems, even if, compared to some other mothers, they were less serious. She seemed to have put aside any thoughts about her illness for the moment, perhaps in order to allow herself to fully enjoy this experience. In reality, throughout our work, I had been rather concerned over her ill health and her fear of mutual damage, but I also reflected on the fact that, at particular times, such as during pregnancy, certain defence mechanisms—such as denial of the seriousness of her state of ill health, or the projection of negative feelings onto the mother-in-law and the safeguarding of her mother's memory—could be very useful as an effective protective strategy. Now Claudia seemed to be aware of her capacity to not want to know and she seemed, at the same time, to fear that this could harm her relationship with her daughter. Perhaps this was precisely the reason for her wanting to continue coming to see me, but my consulting room was too far away because she lived outside the city.

I suggested I might help her to find a colleague located closer to her and I also asked whether she would mind if a child psychotherapy student observed her daughter's development for her first two years, as part of her training. Claudia accepted this second suggestion with great enthusiasm and said she would consider in the future the idea of going to see a colleague.

On reading the observation material some time later, I was greatly struck by a note made by the observer which identified a difficulty on the part of this mother in having physical contact with her baby, who "seemed to be turned in and attached to herself as though from a need to comfort herself". "Giulia slept curled up on the left side of her cot, turned on her left side, sleeping with her little hands crossed, one over the other, and her legs crossed (two months and ten days)". This initial difficulty of physical contact and in holding the baby continued to display itself over time, even when Giulia, having become more independent, tried to crawl towards her mother. The theme of mutual damage seemed to resurface, expressed as a fear of emotional and physical contact, as if mother had some contamination fantasises related to her illness.

However, the gradual bonding process was disturbed by two painful events: Claudia having to undergo surgery on a tumour which was successfully removed and, a few months later, when Giulia was fourteen months old, the news of the sudden death of the consultant who had been looking after her. The observer noted how the mother had been very shaken by this death and had seemed extremely absorbed by her grief, distancing herself emotionally from her daughter.

Perhaps it was not by chance that I saw Claudia again in hospital in the month after the professor's death. She had asked to see me on the same day that she was taking her daughter in for a check-up. It was a hot summer's day and Giulia, then fifteen months old, looked at me with a serious expression from the arms of her mother, who was wearing an attractive blue hat. Claudia's first thoughts were about the consultant, remembering his humility and professional skill, his sensitivity and kindness.

In describing her relationship with her daughter two problem areas emerged, which were closely inter-related but to which Claudia initially seemed not to attribute much importance. The first was her difficulty in making her daughter do as she was told. She said that her daughter was reluctant to spend much time with her and explained that she did not want a child who was too attached to her, she didn't like those children, and, given that she had these problems which caused her to have to be absent, if she were too attached, her daughter would not know how to cope. For this reason since her daughter had been very small she had tended to leave her with friends and other children. What did perhaps worry her somewhat was that recently her daughter had started to have eating problems whereas when she had been little she would eat everything, and she couldn't understand why she didn't seem to have the same problems at school. "At home there is a battle because she wants to be spoon-fed and I refuse and after three hours she's still there and then I get annoyed and I take her plate away. When she doesn't want to do something there's no way round it". The second problem to emerge during our meeting was closely related to this one. Claudia had the impression that her daughter was reasoning like a child much older than her years and, for example, that she was already thinking about marriage. She did not seem to give it much importance because she considered it to be an attitude common to many children these days. However, she said that shortly after having spoken about this ambition, to the amusement of her parents, Giulia had got upset and burst into inconsolable tears, saying that she didn't want to move house when she got married and did not want them to change her bedroom.

We explored her daughter's separation anxiety and connected it to the perception of having a mother who was not well. Claudia pointed out that she never spoke of her illness in her daughter's presence and that it seemed strange that she should pick up her parent's worries. Then, with an expression of profound sadness, she added: "Yes, she always has the future in mind". We reflected on the child's drive to be independent and on how to manage the conflict between the sense of needing to grow up quickly and continuing to suck her thumb. For Giulia it seemed hard to think of being able to grow up slowly and for the mother it was equally difficult to be a parent. She seemed to delegate the function of setting rules to her husband, thus avoiding tensions between her and her daughter, but at the same time she sometimes wanted to step aside to allow her daughter build a strong relationship with her father.

The fear of the perpetuation of mutual damage now concerned the daughter's emotional life. We ended the session with these reflections and with Claudia's request of regular psychoanalytical help.

Conclusion

Previous disappointing experiences, which had been so painful and, at times, dramatic, as to worsen women's feelings of anger and resentment also cast their shadow on the people that were now treating them: the hospital or the gynaecologist is often seen as a parent who has not provided adequate care.

Taking care of yourself is, in effect, an important theme for these women, who will soon have to deal with a child, and their idea of "taking care of oneself" appears to develop precisely through the new perception that someone is taking care of them: it seemed to me that the fact that someone had looked after their emotions and painful feelings had helped them to elaborate in their minds how to relate to their babies.

These women have to face the extremely difficult, emotional task of confronting the profound change required to become a mother, a change which is inevitably accompanied by anxieties and conflicts that these women feel they cannot face alone. Repeated abortions have frozen them in a sort of limbo: they still expect to find a mother who will help them to understand who they are. In other words: "These patients need a kind of mothering and fathering themselves during pregnancy, which can nourish their sense of having good parents within themselves, a basis for health, confidence and optimism and for becoming good parents" (Lewis & Bourne, 2000, p. 56).

Psychoanalytically oriented work is experienced by them as an important recognition by the hospital of the emotional stress they are going through during the new pregnancy. It also helps many of them to contain their fantasies regarding the hospital and doctors and this facilitats the relationship between them.

As we have seen, the emotional difficulties of many women, like their autoimmune problems, are not immediately or readily apparent: in fact, only during the course of the therapeutic intervention did they realize their mental state could be cause for concern and this was also, although not only, due to the possibility that it could be dramatically somatised.

The threat of mutual damage, that is, that the baby's needs might destroy the mother and vice versa, increases their anxiety and it is, in most of these patients, well founded in reality, due to their immune disease. All of this goes against nature, like infertility or the death of a child, and can engender feelings of shame and of guilt for not having provided a fertile ground for the baby's development in the womb. It flies in the face of nature to suggest that the uterus is not a safe place: the baby in the uterus is at risk of being part of this internal world made up of conflicts, anxieties, and defences (Bradley, 2000, p. 30). But often for these women, miscarriages represent distressing proof of the life that they have trouble facing up to, because they highlight the precariousness and pre-existing unreliability of their internal objects.

The deep and painful sense of solitude borne by these women seems to have been attenuated by the possibility of being listened to in a deep, non-judgmental manner, despite this having meant a sometimes very painful and difficult-to-sustain first contact with a different way of seeing things.

In fact, the complexity of the experience of miscarriage makes the women particularly vulnerable. Despite the fact that they have been able to begin to activate positive internal resources, this vulnerability, predictably, has not been radically modified, even after the birth of their children In effect, children born after these difficulties somehow seem, with their particular differences, to grow up a bit too quickly and to be particularly oppositional and independent or excessively dependent. The problem of limits and the separation that is central for many women seems to remerge in this form although at a new level. Even if relieved and happy to have got through such a difficult moment, full of uncertainty and fears, after the birth of their children, these mothers still seem to be bearers of suffering linked to their personal history and their losses. However, most of the mothers that I have treated have been capable of getting in touch with me when they have found themselves in difficulty again and this implies that the intervention has achieved an important preventive objective.

It is therefore necessary to have regular contact with the paediatricians of the mother and baby unit in order to smooth the path for those mothers who feel the need for these support services. The feeling of being able to go forward and not to feel victim to an inexorable destiny—which these women have experienced—and finally managing to bring their pregnancy to term, highlights the importance of being able to plan therapeutic intervention and offer it to all women with high risk pregnancies and also to extend this support to mothers and parents during the first year of life of their child.

If we consider a comment frequently made to these women (and more generally also to people suffering from other diseases)—"You must think positive"—we realise that if we maintain that a positive attitude can help to heal, there is the converse, parallel conviction implicit in the statement which suggests that being unwell may be the result of negativity, pessimism, and anxiety. This invisible, unconscious idea is very frightening because it tends towards the implication that the victim is guilty of her own affliction and it reinforces feelings of inadequacy and a painful sense of guilt.

This is especially true for those women who may be particularly vulnerable and have few emotional resources as a result of the specific dynamics of their internal worlds and weakness of their internal objects. They therefore find working through a loss, or multiple losses, particularly difficult. From the outside these women appear to be, essentially, patients or wives who are overly anxious, but when this translates into something which prevents their ability to procreate, then a different scale of importance is assumed and the reasons for life and, therefore, for the basis of their existence, begin to be questioned.

References

Bion, W. R. (1962). *Learning from Experience*. London: Heinemann Medical (repr. London: Karnac, 1984).

Bradley, E. (2000). Pregnancy and the internal world. In: J. Raphael-Leff (Ed), *"Spilt Milk": Perinatal Loss and Breakdown*. London: The Institute of Psycho-Analysis.

Breen, D. (1989). *Talking to Mothers*. London Free Association Books.

Caplan, G. (1959). *Concepts of Mental Health and Consultation*. Washington, DC: U.S. Children's Bureau.

Garland, C. (1998). *Understanding Trauma*. London: Tavistock Clinic Series.

Hughes, P. (2001). The incidence, correlates and predictors of post traumatic stress disorder in the pregnancy after stillbirth. *British Journal of Psychiatry, 178:* 556–560.

Ingham, G. (1998). Mental work in a trauma patient. In: C. Garland (Ed.), *Understanding Trauma: A Psychoanalytic Approach*. London: Karnac.

Leon, I. G. (1990). *When a Baby Dies*. New Haven, CT: Yale University Press.

Lewis, E. (1979). Inhibition of mourning by pregnancy: psychopathology and management. *British Medical Journal, 2:* 27–28.

Lewis, E. & Casement, P. (1986). The inhibition of mourning by pregnancy: A case study. *Psychoanalytic Psychotherapy, 2(1):* 45–52.

Lewis, E. & Bourne, S. (2000). Pregnancy after stillbirth or neonatal death: psychological risks and management. In: J. Raphael-Leff (Ed), *"Spilt Milk": Perinatal Loss and Breakdown*. London: The Institute of Psycho-Analysis.

Lin, S. X. & Lasker, J. N. (1996). Patterns of grief reaction after pregnancy loss. *American Journal of Orthopsychiatry, 66*: 262–271.

Mancia, M. (1981). On the beginning of mental life in the foetus. *International Journal of Psychoanalysis, 62*: 351–357.

Matthis, I. (2000). Sketch for a metapsychology of affect. *International Journal of Psychoanalysis, 81*: 215–217.

Menzies Lyth, I. (1959). A case study in the functioning of the social system as a defence against anxiety. *Human Relations 13*: 95–121. Reprinted in: I. Menzies Lyth *Containing Anxieties in Institutions: Selected Essays, Vol. 1*. London: Free Association Books, 1988.

Pines, D. (1972). Pregnancy and motherhood: interaction between fantasy and reality. *British Journal of Medical Psychology, 45*: 333–343.

Piontelli, A. (1992). *From Fetus to Child: An Observational and Psychoanalytic Study*. London: Routledge.

Rai, R. & Regan, L. (2006). Recurrent miscarriage, *The Lancet, 368*: 601–611.

Raphael-Leff, J. (1993). *Pregnancy: The Inside Story*. London: Sheldon Press.

Toth, B., Jeschke, U., Rogenhofer, N., Scholz, C., Würfel, W., Thaler, C. J. & Makrigiannakis, A. (2010). "Recurrent miscarriage: current concepts in diagnosis and treatment". *Journal of Reproductive Immunology, 85*(1): 25–32.

Notes

1. Recurrent miscarriage (RM) affects 1–3% of couples but 15% of all clinically recognised pregnancy result in pregnancy failure. At least 25% and probably as many as 50% of all women experience one or more sporadic miscarriages. Known risk factors for RM are genetic, anathomic abnormalities, acquired and inherited trombolphilia, environmental factors, infectious, endocrine 29%, and autoimmune deseases (aPLs 24%, NK 4%). Still 50% remain unknown (Rai & Regan, 2006; Toth et al., 2010).

2. Lupus anticoagulant l.a.c with antiphospholipid antibodies, platelet hyperaggregability and increased resistence uterine arteries.

3. NK cells, Natural Killer, so named because of their capacity to spontaneously kill "foreign" cells such as tumour cells. They play a key role in the development of pregnancy: in a normal pregnancy there are a number of mechanisms which serve to modify the activity of these NK cells in order to allow for the development of a healthy, well vascularised placenta and to support the embryo.

4. Claudia suffered from systemic lupus erythematosus and anti-cardiolipin antibodies and antiphospholipid antibodies.

CHAPTER TWO

The experience of parents of a premature baby

Maggie Cohen

To have an idea of the experience of parents having a premature baby it might be helpful to think about the impact and atmosphere of a neonatal intensive care unit, since almost all babies born more than eight weeks early are likely to spend some time in such a unit. This is the place where parents will get to know and look after their baby in the first days, weeks, or, maybe, months. Added to this there is the fact that, just as with full-term babies, there is no one single experience that all parents of premature babies have. So in writing this chapter I am trying to delineate aspects of life on a neonatal unit that parents will experience in some way and which will affect them. I need to add that I write this as a child psychotherapist who worked in a neonatal unit for some ten years and that I therefore have a particular way of seeing what was going on around me. I want to concentrate on the triangle of babies, parents, and staff in the unit and to see how each element meshes and interacts with the others. I see the babies' experience as being central to all that goes on; however, it may be hard for us to keep this in mind, because of its often traumatic infantile character.

To begin, I will say something about the material setting of neonatal units. These tend to feel rather enclosed and isolated, in some ways to be complete in themselves, hard to get into, and at times emotionally hard to leave. They are rather too warm for comfort for the average adult and crowded, with little room for manoeuvre. The babies' beds are placed close together and the nurses and doctors work around the incubators or cots. Parents fit in to the small amount of space left. The units are quite noisy with alarm bells going off and people talking— sometimes with radios on. It seems that some of this noise is necessary and some unnecessary; what is unnecessary may be there to fill a space into which anxiety might enter. In most units there is the intensive care nursery, or the hot nursery, which is full of technology. Then there is an intermediary nursery and a cool nursery which is more relaxed, the babies can be taken out of their cots and fed and they may still be on a little oxygen but not a ventilator. This is a busy place, with people work- ing in a concentrated and skilled way. When I began my job in a neona- tal unit I often wished that I were a doctor, with a clear task rather than this rather contemplative role. I imagine that parents may sometimes suffer from a similar feeling.

The babies

A multiplicity of equipment surrounds the baby, and tubes and leads are fixed to him, so that it is sometimes hard to focus on the baby in the middle. In the intensive care unit the babies have tubes, which can be heavy, taped to their arms and legs. They breathe artificially by means of a ventilator which is strapped to their nose, and they are mostly fed intravenously. There are bright lights overhead which are occasionally turned down. And there is a constant noise of alarms going off as the babies' oxygen requirements are monitored.

The babies have come too early, their capacities are not fully devel- oped. Their skin is still very thin; sometimes there are fears that it may break down, with primitive and nightmare terrors of what that might mean. The babies are often in pain. Mostly they cannot be picked up by their mothers, although they are sometimes able to be taken out for a cuddle. They are not at home but in a high-tech unit without their mothers being able to protect them from the interventions they need or from the various stimuli invading their senses. They may learn ways of comforting themselves but they need all the support they can get in maintaining these. They have to learn to cope with a diversity of carers as shifts change and new nurses and doctors appear.

It is hard for us to watch these babies. They may be in pain, or be uncomfortable, and they are often being kept alive by machinery. They are not usually being held by their mothers, and we are aware that they do not have their mothers' protection in the way that babies usually do. There is the further difficulty of entering the babies' world and making sense of their movements and their experience. This is both an intellectual and an emotional difficulty. It is hard for us to make sense of the babies' world but it is also something we are often reluctant to do. I think that the sight of these babies, unheld sometimes for weeks and often in pain, puts a strain on the goodness and strength of our own internal world. I think that it is this experience that is at the heart of the life of the unit, and it affects everyone.

I have realised in writing this chapter that I have been reluctant to re-enter the world of the babies that was so familiar to me when I worked in a neonatal unit; even then I would rather find something to do other than watch the babies. I know that in reading a younger colleague's work recently I felt that she was exaggerating the pain endured by the babies. And it has been in reading my own account of the babies in *Sent Before My Time* that I have had to remember and acknowledge what the babies go through. What I am saying is that there is a wish not to see and not to know what the babies feel which afflicts all of us at times. I think that it is hard for us to look at these small, vulnerable babies; they are sometimes exposed to terrible pain which is not mitigated by the mother's body, often not comforted by her voice, and sometimes not held by her eyes and mind because it is virtually impossible for mothers to be with their babies all the time. I think that this engages with our most primitive fears of abandonment and disintegration and that we meet this with fierce defences. Of course, many mothers are there with their babies a lot of the time, but not all can be, and none can be in the way that usually happens with a new born baby.

I will try to give an idea of what the babies' experience may be like by talking about twins, a boy and a girl, who were born at twenty-seven weeks gestation. I first went to see the boy, who I will call John.

> He was lying on his platform, naked, with the ventilator strapped to his mouth. His head was turned to the right, away from the ultra-violet lamp and he was wearing goggles. He had heavy equipment on his arms and legs. He was breathing in a rather laboured way, the breath rippling through his diaphragm. His arms were down

by his sides. His legs flexed open. Then his whole body flexed back. He was squirming and then he was still. He jerked and flexed his right foot. And then he squirmed his whole body up. He put his feet down on the mattress and arched his back. His right foot jerked and his left foot stretched, down and then up. Then his arms stretched up, particularly his left arm. He jerked. Then flexed his right, then left, leg. His legs jerked and then his right arm. Both of his arms were up, his left one against his arm and his right one against the ventilator. His right foot jerked and then he seemed to turn that into stretching and he stretched his whole body with his legs right up and his back curled off the mattress. He yawned and I was aware of his mouth around the plastic. He began to mouth the plastic. His left hand moved against the ventilator. He mouthed the plastic, rested, and then sucked. He was quite still and then began sucking again. He then beat the mattress with a straight right foot.

John was one week old on this occasion. What impressed me was his vulnerability in the middle of all this equipment. There was so much needed to keep him alive and he was so restless. His skin was paper-thin and red and he did not seem at this moment to be able to rest. But he also seemed to be working some things out, for instance, the need his mouth had to suck on something. He sometimes seemed to be just responding to this new environment and sometimes to be beginning to investigate it.

I went on to see his sister. I will call her Emily.

She was under a less strong light and her goggles had slipped down from her eyes. There was a tube in her mouth. Her hands were free and so were her toes. She had a lead to her arm and leads on her legs. But hers did not seem as heavy as John's. Her right arm was down beside her, her fingers were curled and splayed open and touched the tube. Her left arm went up and her hand curled over slightly. Her legs bent up and her right leg slewed across her body to the left. Then she was very still and seemed to go into a deep sleep. Her left toes wriggled a little. She was then still and seemed to have a frown of concentration. Her mouth closed, opened, and stayed open. Her right hand moved slowly far out to the right. This was a gentle, graceful movement. Then her left knee moved up so that it was very bent. A nurse came to check the tubes and Emily hardly moved. Then her left arm moved far out to the left, and again this was very graceful. Her right arm was stretched out to the right. Both arms stretched out at shoulder level.

I felt that she was enjoying her own body, stretching out, exploring her world. Her movements moved me, they were so delicate and graceful, and seemed to be lacking in anxiety. Her mother had told me that the twins had come early because they were too cramped, there was not enough room for them. And Emily here seemed to be enjoying the space.

A nurse now came and put an antibiotic into the tube in Emily's foot. She squirmed and grimaced … and then she suddenly gave a little cry. The nurse pulled the goggles over her eyes, perhaps a bit roughly. She squirmed again and then she was still, but not peaceful in the way that she had been.

Her peaceful time had been interrupted and then a doctor came to take blood to test her oxygen level. Emily heard the doctor and began to squirm, her left leg thrashing, and she arched her back. The doctor had turned the light off and had put on a different one so that she could see what she was doing. The doctor was standing beside Emily, putting on her gloves. She was saying that at any moment she could be called to the labour ward. She said that she felt like a mother with ten children; she could be called at any moment and interrupted in anything that she did. She remembered a job where someone followed her into the toilet and went on talking to her in there. Meanwhile Emily was crying and squirming but was not desperate. The doctor's bleep went off and she had to hurry away. Emily was still. Then she cried a little in a rather pathetic way and moved her shoulders and trunk. She arched her back and went red all over … Emily stretched and whimpered and then her right hand went down and touched her right knee and she was still.

It seemed to me that the space around Emily which had been enjoyable had become different in quality, more persecuting. The doctor was feeling persecuted—that she could not get on with any job without being in danger of interruption, and that she had very few resources and no privacy for recovery. Perhaps Emily felt rather similar. She too was vulnerable to any interruption. She thought, when the doctor came, that she would have the heel prick which would hurt her but it did not happen. So the bit of control and sense that she had of her experience was not confirmed. She seemed to calm herself by touching her right knee with her right hand. She got back some sense of peace. I thought that she tried to escape the bad experience with her arching and going red. As I watched her I felt impressed by her capacity to regulate and comfort herself. I felt that she was working hard to manage her world.

This gives a very small flavour of an ordinary experience on the neonatal unit. We see the babies reach out and try to make sense of their world and at times to retreat from it when it becomes too much. We see the babies learning to cope with pain. One mother told me about how her baby learnt not to cry when the doctor came to take blood and how relieved she was when they came back to an outpatient appointment and he allowed himself to cry when blood was taken. She felt that he no longer had to be so brave.

The families

I now turn to some thoughts about parents. For a mother, this may have been an unexpected early birth. She may have thought that she had a lot longer to go and so may have been unprepared. These last few weeks of having the baby inside may have felt precious to her, maybe a time when she had stopped work and could really concentrate on the new baby and her preparations. Mothers have described to me the shock of going into labour maybe as much as sixteen weeks before the baby was due. And then there is a task of mourning for the baby inside, a baby that has been replaced by a baby outside, with all the anxiety and fear about that.

Or it may be that the mother has been afraid of an early birth. She may have lost other babies and now be threatening to go into an early labour again. Such mothers are often already in bed in hospital, trying to hold on to this baby. I have sometimes been impressed by what a fearful task this is, of how tied the woman may feel to her body, that a trip to the toilet feels so dangerous. She wonders whether getting up and then being in this position will bring on a miscarriage and then whether she will lose the baby down the toilet.

Listening to women talking about these early births, I have been struck by how often there are other stories of loss in their accounts, some experience that may make the mother herself feel dropped. This may be a loss of country or of home. Sometimes there has been a death in the family. Maybe the mother has lost a partner or a parent or other close person. Sometimes the mother may be in prison and the incidence of prematurity in prisons is higher than in the outside population. There may have been a breakdown of the internal and external holding that pregnant mothers seem to need in order to carry their babies.

Once the baby has arrived it is hurried away to the neonatal unit. The unit staff may take a picture of the baby and bring it to the mother. But she is some distance away and not able to hold her baby. When she is able to go to see the baby she will probably be taken in a wheelchair and can see her baby in intensive care. But this is a visit. This is not her home, she is not in control here, either of her environment or of her baby. This is not a criticism of the neonatal unit—they are working hard to save the baby and make him comfortable—but it is how the mother may experience the unit. The birth may well have been more public and less under her control than she was hoping for, and now her coming to her baby is the same. She has to put up with other people making decisions for her baby, other people looking after him and comforting him, and eventually she has to go away, back to her own ward, leaving her baby behind.

So, for a few days she may visit and then it will be time for her to go home. She may have other children at home, who need her, and anyway she is not allowed to stay longer in the hospital. There are some provisions for mothers to stay in the neonatal unit but they are very scant, and it is usually not a possibility unless the baby is either very ill or dying, or for one night before the baby goes home. Nowadays, with bigger neonatal units and fewer local hospitals, home may be a long way away, and occasionally babies have to travel quite far to find a hospital with some space for them. So then the parents have to decide how they are going to manage this. Whatever plan they come up with, leaving the hospital cannot be an easy matter for the mother, packing her bag and walking out without the baby she came in with, leaving him behind in the care of others.

What happens after that will vary tremendously from case to case. If the baby has been very early there will almost certainly be a long spell in the intensive nursery. Many mothers come in daily and learn to do some of their baby's care. But how much they feel able, competent, or welcome to do will depend much on their own inner resources and confidence and on the support that they are given on the unit.

Many women seem to find it useful to talk over their experience with the child psychotherapist and they may use this opportunity in many different ways. Some mothers want to talk near their babies, so as not to be away from them. Sometimes mothers want to go to another room. I have wondered whether that is when they want to talk about their difficult feelings about the baby. Mothers may find themselves having unexpected and unwanted feelings. They may at times find themselves wanting their baby to die, they may want to run away, they may feel paranoid in the unit, thinking that it is an unsafe place. For instance, one mother thought that a mad woman sometimes came into the unit. Or mothers may find themselves hating a particular nurse, and not knowing how to cope with this. In this state of mind it is very hard to leave the unit, and their baby in someone else's care. Mothers may feel burdened with worries, guilt, fantasies, and fears about what brought labour on. They can have difficult feelings about other women in the world, or even in their own families, who have had full-term babies, or well babies, or perhaps just lots of babies. They may be suffering from hatred of their mothers or of their partners. It can be a relief to articulate these feelings in private and, in doing so, to find that these are common, human feelings and not the monstrous and terrible emotions which had been so feared.

At this point I want to mention fathers. It seems to me that their role on the unit can be very difficult. The unit sometimes feels a bit like a womb: warm, busy, crowded, and female. It may be hard for the father to find a comfortable place for himself. Many fathers become interested in the workings of the monitors, as if that is a relief from all of the female concerns. It may also be an antidote to feelings of helplessness and failure at not being able to protect his wife from grief or of not having contributed to making a strong baby. I believe that fathers can easily feel that they have no useful role—they may concentrate on looking after the other children at home and that may be a useful division of labour. But it may then be hard for them to get to know their new baby.

I also want to remember here the baby's siblings who may have all kinds of worries about their new baby, wondering what he looks like, thinking that the grown-ups are worried and that nothing seems quite like it used to be. At times on the neonatal unit we would worry about the siblings. One consultant would remark that reality was usually less worrying than fantasy and that the children should come in. But a neonatal unit is not a particularly child-friendly place, the adults are all busy, there is not much space, and there are fragile babies and delicate equipment around. I mention them here in an attempt to keep these boys and girls in mind.

The staff

This leads me on to thinking about the staff. What has already been hinted at is the intense involvement of the staff in all that goes on in the unit. I think that this work-place poses very particular challenges to the people working there; these people include nurses, doctors, cleaners, secretaries, social workers, child psychiatrists, child psychotherapists, speech and language therapists, and a chaplain. In life we all have our particular moral framework, something that has been built up from our childhood and has been modified by our experience. This informs the ways that we react to things and is linked to what we sometimes call our conscience. This is occasionally challenged in our everyday lives and we have to rethink things. But on the unit the challenges come frequently and often urgently. Staff find that their frameworks may not be adequate to help them "know their own minds"—so they either have to rethink or cling to some ideas that do not quite cover what they are confronted by. It seems to me that this is one reason why staff are quite often in an irritable state. They are being challenged in their own thinking.

Here I enumerate some such situations:

1. There is a baby who is not coping. His skin may be very thin, and it may be becoming more difficult to find a vein to take blood from. He may not be able to come off the ventilator. He may be getting all kinds of infections which would kill him, but he is given antibiotics so he lives. He may have difficulties with his brain which mean that he will not develop. He may be fitting, and overall he may be seen to be in pain. Usually there is a split in the thinking of the staff between those who wish that this baby could die, who feel that it is cruel for him to be kept alive and feel cruel to be involved in this, and those who feel that they are doctors or nurses and that it is their job to keep people alive and that they cannot have ideas about allowing a baby to die.

    I have noticed that each time this debate comes up it is as if all the positions on this spectrum have to be represented and that people may argue in one place with one baby and in another place with another baby. Holding both these responses in mind seems too hard, so people polarise. I think that if we can see that this debate is part of our work, that we need to encompass all of these thoughts, that it is part of the gravity of the work, then we can perhaps manage not to fall out with each other too badly. It is when this split becomes too entrenched that the atmosphere on the unit becomes very difficult.

2. All units seem now to get some premature babies who are born addicted to heroin. These babies are very hard to nurse. They sweat, grunt, and cough, they are hard to settle, and they have a terrible cry which puts everybody's nerves on edge. Once the baby quietens and you think that you have found the thing that will comfort him, often that thing becomes the bad thing that has to be fought against. Nurses are trying to comfort these babies along with other babies in the nursery. They may know the mother because she may have had other babies in the unit and these babies may have been given up for adoption. The nurses may have strong feelings about these addicted mothers. They may compensate by overidentification with the baby or they may feel that they have been dumped with the baby on top of everything else.

3. A mother may be in from a local prison and the staff have to accommodate two wardens on the unit. This may be upsetting to other mothers on the unit and may arouse all kinds of fears and fantasies about what the mother is "in for".

4. There may be mothers in with multiple births—triplets and even quads. And this may challenge some staff members' beliefs about assisted conception.

5. The same is true of the gay couples who are in with a baby. This may challenge the ethical framework of some staff.

Now you may argue that the ethical framework of the staff should be challenged and I am not disputing that. I am merely saying that the unit carries a particularly potent mix of ethical challenges. Most of the staff are women and they are mostly of child-bearing age. They may themselves be having trouble conceiving and may feel provoked by mothers who do not want to keep their own babies. They may be pregnant and have a baby inside who is roughly the same gestation age as the baby they are nursing outside. So the issues on the unit, of fertility, conception, paternity, pregnancy, labour, child care, and death, are likely to be powerful issues for the staff, as indeed they are for all of us.

It seems clear to me that the staff need looking after in this environment. They need a chance to articulate their feelings and to have these respected and listened too. If they do not, they can become rigid in their thinking, or rather thick-skinned in their emotional response and can take their irritability and upset home. I think that a child psychotherapist is in a good position to offer this kind of support to the staff and that this not only helps the staff but the general running of the unit, including the kind of experience that the parents will have.

This brings me on to a consideration of what role a child psychotherapist can have in a unit and what difference his or her presence can make to the parents.

I think that she is there to articulate the babies' experience and to make this available to the staff in thinking about the care of the babies, and to try to keep the babies' experience alive in people's minds at a time when it is tempting to think of them as not having much experience. She should also be available to parents as a safe place where they can articulate their negative, as well as their positive, feelings and to support their need to retrieve their position of primacy with their babies.

I also think that it is useful if she tries to articulate splits amongst the unit staff in an attempt to alleviate this splitting and to provide a place where staff can explore their own negative feelings—be they cruel or murderous—and so not be so burdened by these. There might be all kinds of different ways of providing such a place.

The following is a session by a child psychotherapist, whom I supervised, with a mother whose baby had been on a neonatal unit. The therapist's name is Tess Bailey Sayer and I want to thank her for permission to quote from this session. It is a useful example of what a mother and baby may experience in the unit and of what impact this may have on them afterwards and of how they are helped to think about this.

This was a mother, a nurse, who had had a baby girl, Mandy, who was premature and who had died after four days on the unit. After this the parents had gone for a holiday in Australia and mother had given birth to a second baby, Cindy, within a year of Mandy's death. Tess had noticed that mother blamed herself for Mandy's death and Cindy's early birth. She felt that mother was cruel to herself. She saw her weekly and then fortnightly, and once Cindy was at home it was every two months. This is an excerpt from a session.

> Mother had said that she would not bring Cindy but then had her with her in the waiting room. Mother explained this to the therapist. Cindy was just over a year and Tess noticed that she was looking around the room with curiosity. Mother sat with Cindy on her

lap, facing Tess, and Cindy smiled at Tess, reaching out her hand to her and splaying out her fingers. Mother smiled too and agreed that Cindy had grown and developed. Mother reported that Cindy now recognised and loved her grandparents, that she felt happy and secure with them, she got very excited when she saw them; and that she loved her food now too. And here mother gave her a long puff crisp and sat Cindy on the floor.

Mother went on to say that Cindy had a mind and will of her own and often would not let go of things that she had got hold of. Tess was thinking about how her fighting spirit had probably helped her to survive. And mother went on to say that she slept really well now, all through the night, but that it was hard to get her to sleep. It seemed that she only fell asleep after a huge paddy. And at this point mother looked quite drawn and stressed.

Tess told mother how struck she was by Cindy's struggle against sleep, her wish to hold on to consciousness. She said that it took her back to when Cindy was tiny, having to work so hard to hang on to life, and that perhaps it was this tenacity, the refusal to let go of being here in the world that made the difference for her then, so that now it was still hard for her to allow herself to lose consciousness. The mother stopped what she was doing and looked at the therapist intently. She said that that made sense, that she hadn't thought of it like that. Cindy looked up at the therapist, scanning her face and then smiling and making her smile back. Tess remarked that Cindy seemed to be looking at her to make sure that she was alright.

Mother went on to tell Tess about her plans to go back to work. Cindy would be looked after first by her grandmothers and then she would go to nursery. Mother became very firm in talking about how much Cindy would enjoy nursery and the other children. Then gradually she told Tess how she planned on the first day she left Cindy at nursery not to go to work … her voice trailed off as she said that she knew how upset she would be … how she would not be able to work … Tess said that she was feeling it would be hard to leave Cindy and mother said yes, because when she left her with one of her grandmothers she knew that they love her as much as she did, but that it would not be like that at the nursery. She would have to get to know them and learn to trust them. Cindy had crawled over to the pram and was examining the wheels.

Mother took her away saying that she could not play with that and she put her down near herself. Cindy picked up two toys and knocked one against the other. Mother said, smiling at her, that she liked noise. Tess remarked that, although she would be taking a one-year-old to nursery, this might be taking her back to when she was tiny and to all the separation they had had to deal with then, when neither of them were ready for it, and the old feelings might be coming up again. Mother nodded tearfully, saying that she thought when she took Cindy in for the first few times, she would stay with her, to help her settle and that people might think that she was being overprotective in this. Tess said that it sounded as though it was hard to sort out what was helpful to Cindy and what might hold her back. Mother nodded vigorously and said ruefully that her husband thought it was a shame that she had to go back to work. She got out a cup of milk with handles on each side and passed it down to Cindy who grasped the handles firmly and took a few gulps too quickly and suddenly found herself gasping for breath, an alarmed expression on her face. She let go of the cup with one hand trying to recover herself and looking up at Tess. Tess said "Oh dear, are you choking Cindy?" and mother commented to her that too much had gone in and asked her if she were alright. She took a tissue and wiped Cindy's chin and Cindy resumed drinking, put the cup down, and went on playing. Tess then said to mother that she wondered if she was feeling a bit of a push to get on with this, to hurry it along but that in fact there was no hurry and that it would not set her back in her progress if she needed a bit more time at home with her grandmothers or with mum. Mother asked Tess if she really thought that and she said that she did. She said that they had only quite recently reached this settled, happy patch at home with Cindy being well. She went on to talk about what a huge step it was to go to nursery and that it was a different and, in some ways, artificial environment with so many little ones all together. Mother was looking thoughtful and said that it was hard to get the balance right. Tess said that the good thing was that Cindy was no longer the tiny scrap that she had been and that she was good at letting mum know what she wanted and what she felt about things. Mother looked at Cindy and laughed. Mother then began to think about how she might work all of this out.

Mother told Tess about Cindy getting her first cold and how she had not been worried but that her husband's mother had panicked and so she had gone to the GP but that she knew that she did not need to.

Mother then went on to talk about how she felt about other women's pregnancies and how easy it was for them to get pregnant. She said bitterly that she and her husband waited until she was twenty-four weeks to announce her pregnancy and then her waters broke. She talked about her feeling that the world was full of pregnant women and how jealous she was of them because she knew that she was not going to have another baby. (Here, when mother began to cry, Cindy looked up from her play and then back down again.) The consultant had said that she could try again. But she knew that they did lose Mandy and they might have lost Cindy, and they knew what Cindy had been through and that she might not have ended up in such good shape. So they might have a child with special needs and that that would not be good for Cindy. Mother would not be prepared to put another baby through what Cindy had been through. Also, she knew now that she would never have an ordinary pregnancy and birth. The first part of the pregnancy with Mandy was lovely but it was not with Cindy. It was pretty awful all the way through. Tess talked to her about all of this mourning. And Mother talked about the pleasure of watching Cindy now and realising what she had missed with Mandy. Tess said that it was likely that this mixture of feelings would be around right the way through to having grandchildren. Mother told her of a woman she had met who was sobbing at the school gate when her little girl had just started. People thought she was crying because of her little girl but she told Mother that she was crying about her little boy baby who had never got to school. Cindy came over and held on to mother's leg and mother asked her if she wanted to come up. Cindy stood on Mum's lap looking over her shoulder into the reflective window, then she looked round at Tess with mouth and eyes wide open and then turned to her mum. Mum said that when she is upset she is aware that Cindy watches her and then she told her that she was upset but she was alright. As Mother and Tess went on talking Cindy began putting her fingers inside mother's mouth and nose in a sharp way, leaning away from her with an air of detached interest. Mother turned her head away continuing to talk to Tess. When she turned back, Cindy patted her cheek then poked more fingers up mum's nose, holding her cheek with the other hand. Mother said that she often did this and it was a real pain! Tess said that it seemed that Cindy wanted Mum to know what it felt like to have things come and poke into your nose and mouth in a sharp way. Mother laughed in recognition and said yes and there was no getting away from it. Cindy's fingers pursued her as she tried to get away from them. And Tess talked to her about this being about Cindy's recovery, which is happening alongside her own, that Cindy too had experiences that she needed to process, but for her, much of her experience and memory will be in her body, so she is using her body to let her mum know about this so that she can help her with this.

The session came to an end and Mum and Tess made another time to meet.

I was struck by the movement of this material. Mother brought Cindy with her, ostensibly because they were going on to a physio appointment, but also maybe because mother wanted Tess to see Cindy and to attend to some baby feelings in both baby and mother. She certainly wanted to talk about what a strain bedtime was. Tess linked the problem now with some strengths around Cindy's early coping. And then mother goes on to talk about going back to work. She puts on a firm voice but quickly shows how painful this is for her. Tess intervenes in a rather unusual way to say rather clearly that she does not think Cindy needs to go to nursery yet. I thought that she felt encouraged by mother reporting father as saying that it was a shame for Cindy to go yet and then by Cindy choking over the milk coming too quickly. Again she makes a link back to their neonatal experience and expresses her own view of nurseries being rather artificial places. It seemed that Tess fell into a motherly role to mother, supporting her in her mothering.

Mother then seemed to split off her more anxious self into her mother-in-law who was so worried about Cindy's cold. This seems to lead Mum on to talk about her own more hidden feelings about other women's pregnancies and her sadness at not having another baby. She seems to be describing a loss of innocence, that she knows too much now to be able to embark on this, that she could not put another baby through this. And she links this to her grief about her own dead baby and the feeling that this will always be with her in some way.

Cindy seemed conscious of all this going on, aware of the gravity of the conversation between Mother and Tess. But then when Mother began to weep it seemed to spark off her own unprocessed experience and she poked her fingers into her mother. With her knowledge of the neonatal unit Tess immediately saw this connection and made it for Mum, who then also saw it and could then be less persecuted by it. And she could then help the process of Cindy's bodily experience being given words. Besides this, I thought that there is for both Mother and Cindy the temptation of using cruelty as a relief from pain; so mother takes on a rather hard voice when she talks about sending Cindy to school and Cindy, in communicating her own experience of being intruded upon, is also perhaps hurting Mother for intruding into her with her tears.

It seems to me that the child psychotherapist here holds the early experiences of the baby in mind and makes the links that help the mother to be able to make sense of the baby at the time. As I said at the beginning, all parents of premature babies have different experiences. I saw a mother recently who had had a twenty-three week gestation baby, who felt that she had retained her role as the person who knew her baby best and who felt cushioned in her experience by the close presence of her husband and mother. But even she began to weep as she embarked on telling me the story of those first few weeks and months. I think that as professionals it is important that we realise how hard this experience can be so that when we see a child who has been born prematurely we realise something of what the family has been through.

As I described at the beginning, neonatal units can be rather isolated places, cut off from other parts of the hospital. In a similar way I think that parents of premature babies can become isolated in their experience of their babies' prematurity. The time in the unit can be absorbing and can take the mother, and maybe both parents, away from outside life. So they can become cut off from friends, family, and a wider social life, which they need to support them. I think that this is partly because what they are going through is so time-consuming and absorbing. But it is also because the experience itself is so difficult. It is painful to be separated from your baby, it can be excruciating not to be able to protect your baby from its own early infantile experience, and it is hard work to process and bear the high levels of anxiety, often anxiety that the baby will die or be very damaged. Added to this is the fact that the unit itself can be a challenging and painful place for the staff and so they are having to struggle with their own feelings. Of course, this often leads to powerful feelings between the staff and the parents and babies, feelings that involve all concerned in emotional, intellectual, and practical work, often accompanied by a deep sense of gratitude, affection, and respect as well as more negative responses. All of this can take some recovering from for all participants. In this chapter I have tried to describe this and to show how a child psychotherapist tries to support that recovery.

CHAPTER THREE

Emotional turmoil around birth

Hendrika C. Halberstadt-Freud

The time before and after the birth of a baby is heavily loaded with emotions. Especially with the first child, as a relationship of two persons becomes a threesome. Great adaptations are required of both partners. The mother is preoccupied with her baby and the father might feel excluded. The young mother can feel trapped in a situation from which no turning back is possible. "Once a mother always a mother" makes her anxious. A man can walk away, a woman can't as easily. A mother will harbour many fantasies and dreams about the unborn baby. She might be more exuberant or more anxious, for a large part depending on her relationship with her own mother. Being a mother transcends the generations, as styles of mothering are transmitted from mother to daughter. The puerperium, meaning the period around being pregnant and giving birth, implies risks as well as chances to find a new equilibrium. When emotional problems do arise, the possibility exists to reconsider many feelings as the sluices are open during the time around birth.

There is a risk of depression involved, but the positive message is: things can be changed for the better. If required, both mother and child will benefit from psychological help around pregnancy.

Emotional support is important, from partner, mother, or professional.

Reactions after giving birth vary. There are the so-called postpartum blues and spells of crying which, if not too serious, will pass. Some anxieties around mothering and the well-being of the baby are normal, especially with a first child. In that case the mother might need some ongoing therapeutic help to prevent harm to her and her child's development. Some mothers, however, have more serious reactions after giving birth. They cry a lot and are depressed and confused to the point of hating their child, wanting to kill him. This is a psychotic reaction which requires intervention. Medical treatment with anti-psychotics and possibly hospitalisation is called for. Current estimates are that about one mother in ten experiences some form of neurotic depression after giving birth (Gavin et al., 2005) and one in one hundred become psychotic, but definitive data are still lacking. Postnatal depression in its varied manifestations has not received the attention that it deserves. Psychiatry has always dealt with the most severe cases, but the less serious cases are still mostly neglected. Psychological insight in this condition is still limited. Pospartum pathology is often considered purely hormonal or physical and not treated appropriately. Traditionally in psychoanalysis, motherhood and the early mother–child relations have been studied from the infant's side, the fantasies and feelings of the mother often remaining a "dark continent".

A review of the literature reveals how little has been published about the psychological treatment of postpartum depression. This chapter offers a way of looking at the phenomenon from a theoretical and practical point of view.

It is proposed here that separation and individuation are not only an important phase in the life of the child but are also highly significant from the mother's point of view. I suggest that the woman's unresolved symbiotic illusion (Freud, H., 2011) with her own mother can play a central role in postpartum depression.

Three clinical cases are presented here to illustrate the therapeutic interventions that are possible. The first and the third cases, Ernestine and Clare, concern a psychoanalysis of three to five sessions a week. The second case, Lavinia, was in once-a-week psychotherapy plus antidepressant medication. The case of Ernestine illustrates the clinical and theoretical implications of a transgenerational perspective on postnatal depression. Clare was in analysis because of manifold problems and, it only turned out during her treatment, that she had also experienced a postnatal depression.

I will introduce two theoretical concepts and their interaction, the first being the "symbiotic illusion" used as a defence mechanism (Halberstadt-Freud, 1989, 1991; Freud, H., 2011); the second being multigenerational involvement in pathology such as postnatal depression.

Pregnancy and giving birth

Regression threatens every new developmental phase of the female life cycle, as progression means renewed identification with the maternal figure. The events of pregnancy and giving birth not only mean following in the mother's footsteps but also imply identification with the baby (Benedek, 1973; Bergler, 1959; Deutsch, 1945; Hayman, 1962; Pines, 1982). Renewed symbiotic phantasies in relation to the mother stir old wishes of fusion with her and concomitant fears of re-engulfment. In other words, approach–avoidance conflicts, typical of the so-called rapprochement phase of infant development, are common in the puerperium. After delivery, the loss of oneness with the baby can give rise to separation fears, ambivalence, and regression in the mother. Emotional regression and identification with the "oral existence" of the crying baby can lead to jealousy of the infant. A severe superego and identification with the powerful, feared, and punishing mother figure, leads to self-reproach and depressive feelings. The fear of being a bad mother may bring about the impulse to kill either oneself or the baby. The baby may be seen as a monster threatening to metaphorically eat up the mother and consume her whole life. Guilt feelings about these hostile feelings tend to be projected, and, as in Ernestine's case, the husband gets blamed for not providing the love and attention the puerperal woman missed from her maternal object in the past as well as in the present.

The temporary regression implied in the "primary maternal preoccupation" (Winnicott, 1956/1958) can endanger a woman's equilibrium. She has to assume her maternal role and she must be able to identify with the needs of the baby in order to be able to take care of the infant. The revived desire to be a baby herself has to be repressed and denied. In Ernestine's case, she resented the baby who once more forced her to take responsibility instead of fulfilling her wish to be taken care of herself. She tried to banish her envy and hatred of the baby, who upset her entire life, by reaction formation. This implied overdoing it and being more solicitous and caring than normally required. Ernestine became the more than perfect mother and exhausted herself completely. Her mother became more demanding while her baby needed her constant attention. As a consequence, she felt pulled in two directions. Analysis helped her to be freed from the inner conflicts around the responsibility she felt for the well-being of her mother. The mother was unconsciously competing with the baby and threatening to die if she did not get the attention she demanded from her daughter. Thanks to the treatment, Ernestine became able to withstand her mother's claims and realised for the first time how much she hated her for being so demanding.

The woman who becomes a mother is strongly confronted with her inner mother, the maternal image she carries inside herself from childhood onwards. In postnatal depression, she mourns the mothering she missed. She is afraid her aggression will kill her mother so she has to divert her anger and directs it at herself, her partner, or her child.

The illusion of being one with the mother, crumbles during the puerperium. The pact is broken, and hostility, so far safely split off and projected onto the outside world (e.g., the father)—threatens to re-enter consciousness. This shattering of the false idyll with the mother, at a time when emotional support is needed in becoming a mother herself, can easily prompt a breakdown. A "mother phobia" or "allergy" can result, expressed in fears such as of having the mother near, an aversion to touching her or being touched by her, and generally a need to keep her at a distance. This is illustrated by Clare's case. The mother is not allowed to approach the baby, or else … evil will happen, a theme which often surfaces in fairy tales, involving evil stepmothers or wicked-fairies.

Separation between mother and daughter is always an important theme for every female. How much do I identify with my mother, how much individuation is possible or desirable? Here male and female development differs. Though the gender identity of a girl is not threatened by her close tie with her mother, there are other pitfalls. Individuation and separation is made more difficult by the absence of sexual difference. While a girl is born in a homosexual relationship, a boy starts his life in a heterosexual one. Here biology is destiny. Moreover, female development is a multigenerational event along the maternal lineage, as we will see in the case of Ernestine. Mothering styles are directly transmitted from (grand) mother to daughter. If the developmental milestones around separation and individuation have failed to take place, a woman has more chance of falling prey to a post-natal depression. After giving birth, the daughter is confronted with her ambivalent feelings toward her mother. The dyadic bond with the mother becomes problematic.

Clare: resentment and conflicts towards her mother

Clare sought treatment because of manifold problems with her "intrusive" mother. She came from a very strict puritanical background. Her mother was an unbending character who was rather domineering towards her daughter. Clare hated her because she always made unpleasant and critical remarks. To outsmart her mother, who was very stiff and tight-laced, she married a man who was totally the opposite. He was sloppy and knew, unlike Clare, no shame feelings. He dressed completely nonchalantly notwithstanding his profession, which demanded some respectability. The marriage was not conflicted; the husband accepted Clare unconditionally, notwithstanding her sexual inhibitions. She had great difficulty reaching orgasm. She had the phantasy that her mother lay under her bed and could hear what happened while she made love. When she criticised her mother during treatment sessions she had the feeling her mother was sitting in the corner, listening. Her ten-year-old daughter, Lisa, was a difficult child. After she was born, Clare had been in total panic about how to handle the baby. Instead of asking advice, she tried hard to ban her mother, as if she was a dangerous fairy who could damage the baby. Her aversion was so strong that she became unable to touch her mother or be touched by her. This aloofness between them replaced her former pseudo-closeness. Lisa became her idol instead. She admired the baby beyond all reasonable bounds. Her ambivalent feelings became split between the bad mother and the ideal baby. However, mixed feelings toward Lisa showed in her not being able to use baby sounds and baby talk. Clare raised the baby in complete silence while observing her in total fascination. The situation must have been pretty tense for both of them. Clare felt guilty when Lisa cried, as if her mother lay in the crib accusing her of negligence. She always felt guilty and was never a good-enough mother. She became obsessed with the idea that she must be the ideal mother and her baby must be perfect. Clare, who was ambitious and well-educated, had always made great demands on Lisa. She imagined the child to be a genius. She tried to teach her to talk, and later to read and to write, at a much too early age. The child had to be smart and verbal at a developmental stage where this was still not possible.

Infants react to stress with physical symptoms such as cramps, sleeplessness, etc. Rather than being perfect, Lisa developed serious digestive problems. She got a special diet, which required the withholding of the foods she liked best. This caused Lisa to become an angry child, as she always felt wronged and frustrated by her mother. The situation became even more complicated when Clare had a second daughter, although she was more relaxed this time. Lisa became extra jealous, as her sister was allowed food that was forbidden her. Clare's unconscious sadism towards her mother was projected onto her first child, not the second one. Lisa reacted to this and once, during the analysis, even threatened her mother with a knife.

The analysis was successful in the sense that the relationship with Lisa became a positive one and Clare's sexual problems were more or less resolved. She had academic success and was content with the results of the treatment. Her mother did not change her attitude, but Clare became more separated from her and the relationship normalised without being close.

Lavinia: a traumatic birth

Lavinia seeks treatment because she has felt tense and depressed since the birth of her first child, now one year old. About her background she tells me that her parents always had a tense relationship. They finally divorced when she was fifteen years old. Lavinia, a gifted and beautiful woman, has a tense relationship with her husband, which became more so around her pregnancy. He, too, comes from a rather troubled family, his parents having divorced when he was still a small child. Alas, old patterns tend to repeat themselves over the generations. After delivery, Lavinia feels lonely and left alone by her mother and her husband. She is angry inside, but she is unable to express her grievances and ask for the support she needs. Her anger, instead of being expressed, is turned inward and she becomes very sad and depressed.

Lavinia walks the streets for hours with her child in the pram and she cries. She is clearly suffering from a post-natal depression. After a long delay, she decides to seek professional help and comes to me for once-a-week therapy. Her problems are dealt with, combining anti-depressants and talking about her hardships and complaints. Her obsessional and perfectionistic character, and the circumstances around birth, make this a very difficult period for her. The delivery was difficult, she tells me, due to an inexperienced midwife who gave the wrong instructions at the final moments. She was traumatised, physically and emotionally. Her genital area became injured and painful, due to a too-sudden birth. Problems with breastfeeding followed. She tried very hard, persevering for hours. She exhausted herself but was unsuccessful. This was a grave disappointment for her. Lavinia is bothered more by her perfectionism since work and care of the baby have to be combined. She has a hard time of it and it takes an effort from both herself and her therapist to get things moving in the right direction again.

Lavinia was, for a long time, unable to make contact with her daughter because she was too distraught. She did not consciously hate the child, but unconsciously blamed her for the emotional and physical damage she had caused. At the same time, Lavinia felt deeply guilty about her lack of love and enjoyment of her daughter. The child was never satisfied and could scream so loudly that it was hard to bear, until she got what she wanted. She became a demanding toddler who wanted to eat all the time and even grabbed the food from her mother's plate. She developed contactual problems and used to turn her head away when approached. It took Lavinia at least a year to become less depressed. She tended to feel guilty about the times she could not feel love for her child and only functioned mechanically. Admitting anger towards her mother helped to resolve the hostility she felt towards her child. During treatment, the relationship with the child gradually improved and the depression was lifted. Eventually she was able to find a new equilibrium.

Ernestine: a symbiotic illusion

When Ernestine is referred for analysis, she is thirty-seven years old and has a four-month-old boy. She looks extremely worried and run down. She is casually dressed, looking more like a boy than a mature woman, suggesting that her sexual identity is conflicted. To her great dismay, her life changed totally after giving birth to a baby who had not been planned.

Ernestine is inconsolable and cries for hours every day, without understanding what is the matter with her. She tells me she feels intermittently desperate and angry. When she realised she was pregnant, she considered an abortion without informing her partner. Later she changed her mind and decided she wanted to keep the baby. Now she fears she is a bad mother who does not take proper care of her baby. She once had the murderous fantasy of throwing her baby out of the window. She worries a lot about what he eats, whether it is safe or poisonous, she even fears poisoning him with her milk. She is obviously afraid of her own aggressive impulses.

Though Ernestine and her partner have lived together for over twenty years (not married) she never consciously wished for a child and seldom gave motherhood a thought.

Ernestine's mother has always warned her not to become pregnant. She used to tell her daughter what an unpleasant and depressing experience pregnancy had been for her, the suggestion being that, as a baby Ernestine might have harmed her mother. This must have created a feeling of not being welcome. As a consequence she became a very demanding and clinging toddler. Not surprisingly, being this "monster" not only fostered a profound sense of guilt in the patient but it also made her angry. This anger could not be acknowledged, for fear of being even more rejected.

Ernestine's conflicts around femininity have always found expression through physical symptoms. Anxiety, stress, and emotional pain played out via the body. During menstruation, she habitually suffered heavy headaches which, she insists, have nothing to do with emotional problems, but are purely physical. It came as a great surprise to her that being pregnant gave her a feeling of exhilaration. She felt, for the first time, as if she was a superwoman and a super-mum, proudly showing off her pregnancy and swinging her heavy belly around for everybody to see. The shock after delivery was all the greater. The physical separation from her baby made her feel empty, flat, lonely, and totally deprived. Since his birth she has been mourning her lost unity with the baby.

Unacknowledged feelings of ambivalence toward her mother, Mrs. A., surfaced for the first time during Ernestine's pregnancy. She is disappointed by her mother's negative reaction to the baby and her total lack of support that she, as a young mother, needs. Instead, her mother seems to feel strong rivalry with the baby and the attention he gets. She has become very demanding, is often ill and in need of special care. Ernestine is unable to show her mother any anger. Instead of setting limits to her mother's demands Ernestine directs her anger at her partner. She admits being chronically and unreasonably angry with him. Although he is a caring father and a helpful partner, she feels lonely, as if neglected by him instead of by her mother. She fights him wherever she can and claims his attention as never before. They fight about every detail of their daily life and particularly around issues concerning food. She makes a scene when she thinks he might use food that is beyond the sell-by date. She is preoccupied with the question of when to throw food away in order not to be poisoned by it. Concerning the care of their son, she is sure she knows best and leaves no room for the father, who might do him harm or even poison the child. Although she can be argumentative and vindictive, she is mostly passively pouting, complaining, and crying. She feels oppressed and victimised. As this couple had been quite happy when they lived together before the patient's pregnancy, the change has been striking and is clearly connected to the baby's arrival.

During the analysis the negative feelings Ernestine has towards her mother, who is not at all pleased with her grandchild, are quickly becoming manifest for the first time.

Although Ernestine is desperate enough to agree to my proposal of analysis, she insists that she doesn't have any problems, while tears pour out of her eyes, demonstrating a clear tendency toward splitting and denial. From the start of her analysis, her ambivalence about being a mother is clear. On the one hand, she defensively idealises motherhood and makes excessive demands on herself. On the other hand, "being opposed to the role of women in our society", she rejects her femininity. In her present predicament, she "feels hooked and a slave".

Ernestine's anger about the fact that having a child has changed the course of her life, dissipates quickly in the first few months of analysis. Having a son seems to have become a boost to her self-esteem. She considers him almost as a part of her own body and his well-being gratifies her sense of self-worth as a mother. Problems with mothering usually go back several generations. The maternal lineage is especially well-suited to the perpetuation of either positive or negative attitudes being transmitted from mothers to daughters, such transmission being apparently less strong when the child is a son. A male child does not automatically inherit the angry feelings of the mother towards her mother. Ernestine is very relieved that her child is a boy and not a girl, enabling her to have positive feelings towards him. During the analysis she quickly changes into an overprotective, solicitous mother who loves and enjoys her baby.

Ernestine's psychoanalytic treatment confirms my experience with other postpartum patients and the literature on this subject. She struggled with her femininity and was apprehensive of the combined roles of wife, lover, and mother. Her destructive feelings were for the most part not directed at the baby but at her partner and at herself. She became more dominating toward her partner as she felt herself to be a victim after the birth of her baby. Puerperium put a heavy burden on her habitual defences—denial, splitting, projective identification (projecting denied or unwanted traits into the other and identifying with him or her), and reaction formation. She temporarily lost her psychic equilibrium. Her former ego-strength was gone. Her increased masochism masked the fact that she felt a strong need to be in control, and she began to make use of obsessional mechanisms. She became simultaneously more dependent and more aggressive. Trying to be a perfect mother, she exhausted herself and landed in a downward spiral.

The analysis was effective in undoing the old balance and finding a new one. Among other things, it helped her to give up mothering her mother without a renewed psychic breakdown after her next pregnancy.

Multigenerational links and symbiotic illusion

Linking my work with the existing literature, I want to suggest two points. First the need for multigenerational involvement in health as well as in pathology, especially between mothers and daughters. The second point regards symbiosis and what I have called the symbiotic illusion (Halberstadt-Freud, 1989), which can play a vital role in postnatal depression.

Mothers form an essential link in the carry-over from one generation to the next. Motherhood is a three-generation experience, accompanied by a revival of past conflicts and anxieties (Pines, 1972). The feminine lineage, by its strength and direct carry-over and without the intervention of gender differences, makes it easy to pass on assets as well as weaknesses.

The primordial homosexual bond between mother and daughter can have powerful effects on female development. "The relation between mother and daughter is handicapped from the start … due to the sexual identity between mother and daughter" (McDougall, 1970, p. 98). Girls are born in a same-sex relationship in which a woman creates her own likeness by having a daughter. She projects herself more easily into a daughter than into a son. Mutual identification creates more closeness, more ambivalence, more hatred, and more longing for maternal love in women. "The roots of feminine erotism are laid down in early infancy" (McDougall, 1986, p. 228). Women struggle with the problem of how to integrate the profound homoerotic tie to their mother. The need for a girl to identify with her mother, added to her being of the same sex and gender, breeds likeness and the consequent illusion of sameness. Moreover, it is important to remember that a woman's reaction to her offspring has to be seen in the context of her mother, and of her grandmother. The therapist has to take at least three (possibly four) generations along the maternal lineage into account when interpreting pathology such as post-natal depression.

Symbiosis, as Mahler (1968) admitted, is not meant literally, as mutual dependence, when used to describe the normal mother–child situation. "The term symbiosis is a metaphor. It does not describe, as the biological concept of symbiosis does, what actually happens between two separate individuals. The essential feature of symbiosis is the delusion of a common boundary of the two actually and physically separate individuals" (1968, p. 9). The baby, in his or her illusion of omnipotence, can imagine being one with the mother and partaking of her greatness and power, but normally mothers do not depend on their babies as a support for their narcissism, as is the case in pathology.

The idea of symbiosis is an imaginary ideal from the child's point of view. "Blissful symbiosis" is an idealised view of the baby's feelings. There is no evidence of a positive symbiotic phase (Brody, 1982). According to Stern the baby is not fused with the mother in the sense of not having boundaries: "the experience with a self-regulating other ... does not breach or confuse the sense of core self and a core other" (Stern, 1985, p. 105).

A two-sided dependency, a pathogenic reciprocal symbiotic illusion, not at all rare between mothers and daughters, is a defence mechanism and a serious sign of disturbance.

The "imaginary baby"—the mother's phantasies about her unborn baby—is a normal phenomenon. It becomes pathological when a mother harbours the phantasy that all her unfulfilled desires and aspirations will be met by her baby. If a mother is insecure, narcissistically vulnerable, and/or depressed, she risks losing sight of the real baby and its needs. She tends to imagine the child as part of her physical and emotional self, and as indispensable to her well-being. She cannot see it as a separate person with needs of his or her own. A situation arises in which she needs the baby to need her, as is seen in sleep disturbances of baby's (Lebovici, 1983). Becoming a mother, and having power over a child, can give rise to a perverse mother–child relationship, for example, a symbiotic illusion, where the mother perverts her love for the child into a self-serving relationship.

In these cases, the mother needs constant confirmation that she is the good, beloved parent. She demands likeness and sameness—for instance, she may believe the infant to be hungry when she, herself, is. As we shall see, this situation arises when a mother is not separated but still merged with her own internal maternal imago. She tends to use her baby, from his or her birth onwards, as a transference object on whom she projects her fears and hopes—in fact her image of herself as a baby.

Ernestine alternates between being identified with her crying baby (Blum, 1978; Zachary, 1985), representing herself, and seeing her child as an accusatory figure representing her guilt-inducing mother. As Ernestine felt accused by her mother, she now feels blamed by her crying baby. She hates her child for any sign of independence or autonomy, signifying separation, and she is unable to confront her hatred. But gradually, anxious that he might die, she replaces her wish to get rid of him and becomes overprotective—a reaction formation which on the one hand indicates the strength of her hatred at her mother/child, but on the other also indicates her capacity to love and protect her baby.

Mothers like Ernestine resent their child and feel threatened by its demands unless "blissfully" merged in a mythical union over which she has full control. Consequently, they cannot afford to allow anything resembling separation or individuation to take place

Their infantile primary homosexual bond with their own mothers persisting in the unconscious has not allowed their Oedipus complex and their relationship to men to develop properly. Males are resented as disturbers of the homosexual bond with the mother. These women remain caught up in a dyadic rather than a triadic relationship. For a mother such as Ernestine, merging with her mother or her child remains a lure and a threat. Her heterosexuality is weakly developed. As her father has played a minor role in her life, so does her husband, especially after the birth of a child. As a mother, she tends to become totally involved in her baby, without a life of her own and without interests other than for her child. The child senses this symbiotic need of the mother and, for emotional survival, the child tries to comply. Locked in a symbiotic idyll, the mother, as well as the daughter, has a vital interest in keeping up the illusion of a happy bond, for which they pay a high price. As we know, being "condemned to each other" fosters hostility that has to be suppressed and denied. As a child, she misses out her pubertal protest against her mother who is unable to set limits. If she becomes critical of her mother, she fears she will kill her by the sheer wish to separate from her. These deeply held beliefs are, to an extent, unconsciously passed on through the generations and therefore shared—and confirmed—between mother and daughter. For instance, another patient who also came to analysis suffering from post-natal depression, had succeeded in confronting her mother and being critical of her for the first time in her life. The following day, her mother, who had been severely depressed for a long time, committed suicide. The daughter felt she had murdered her mother, and at the same time the mother's suicide can be seen as a desperate punishment for her daughter's attempt to be independent.

An increase in guilt feelings is to be expected when autonomy is experienced as hostility. Disavowal of anger and frustration can lead to splitting and projection of the negative feelings outside of the dyad. Because the father's image tends to be excluded, he can easily become the receptacle of hostile phantasies, especially because mother and child will do everything to keep their false idyll intact.

In this family constellation, where the father keeps his distance and the mother needs repeated proof that she is a good mother, she provides love and care on condition that the child gives up its independence. This is illustrated in Marcel Proust's famous novel *Remembrance of Things Past*. He describes a goodnight kiss episode in which the mother "abdicates" by giving in to her son's childish wishes. The boy is desperately crying, as he cannot go to sleep without a long session of kissing with his mother. He is so wretched that she decides to give up her demands on him and gives in to his wish to be consoled. She spoils him, on condition that he gives up his independence. Her "abdication" means that he will remain forever tied up to her, and to her mother, the narrator's beloved grandmother. "It struck me that my mother had just made a first concession ... that it was a first abdication on her part from the ideal she had formed for me, ... that I had succeeded ... in relaxing her will ... and that this evening opened a new era ..." (Proust, 1981, p. 41). She spends the night with her son and the father goes to bed alone (Halberstadt-Freud, 1980, 1991); a false and perverse mother-son idyll is created which will mark forever the child's future love life (Welldon, 1989).

In the symbiotic illusion, mother and child strike an unconscious deal to oblige one another in endless "bartering" (Khan, 1962/1979). As described in Proust's brilliant example, the child may become a willing partner, requesting and offering to mother exclusive dependence and blurring of boundaries. When tokens of dependence are not given by the child, maternal love turns into hatred. The result is "symbiotic anxiety", with its archaic fears of either loss of identity through fusion with mother or loss of love. For the daughter, having a baby of her own breaks the spell with the mother and the resulting confusion may end in post-natal depression.

The difficulty in separating from her mother hinders the daughter in forming a triadic relationship. She remains in a dyad with her mother. When she becomes a mother, she feels burdened by two competing dyadic bonds, one with her mother and the other with her child. Her husband, a denigrated object like her father, is not allowed, or is unable, to alleviate her plight. Her (internal) mother figure is imagined as envious and demanding, in competition with the baby. She tries to solve this conflict by hating either her mother, her baby, or herself, as was the case with Ernestine. Identification with the baby and its crying gave rise to an intensification of her own baby wishes and desires vis-à-vis her (internal) mother. Under the influence of reaction formation, Ernestine turned hatred into loving care. She became so utterly devoted that she became mentally and physically exhausted.

Discussion and conclusions

The period around childbirth, called puerperium, is a period of rapid transitions allowing for change through therapeutic intervention. The bodily and emotional turmoil of the woman before and after childbirth increases her sensitivity and opens up chances for psychological change as a new equilibrium has to be found. It can be considered the third separation/individuation phase of women, after the very early stage and adolescence, offering an opportunity to reinforce dependency or to develop autonomy. In the period after delivery the emotional sluices are wide open, creating possibilities for renewed personal growth. The puerperium can not only be a period of regression but of progress as well. My patients succeeded in resolving their rapprochement (approach-avoidance) conflicts enabling them to loosen the ties with their maternal object. Massive anger at the mother became conscious and was partially worked through in the transference.

The suffering of mother and child would justify devoting more attention to postpartum depression than the subject has received from psychoanalysis so far (Anthony, 1983; Asch, 1966; Asch & Blum, 1978; Fraiberg, 1980; Rubin, 1974). This fact has its historical roots. The Oedipus complex was conceived according to male development. If the founder of psychoanalysis had been a woman, she might have chosen Electra as an example of female pathology instead of Oedipus. For women, the fateful combination of love and hate for the same object is the kernel of conflicts, so well expressed in the eternal myth of Electra.

For a long time, female development was understood in the light of drive development and the Oedipal stand vis-à-vis the father, to the detriment of the study of the mother–daughter relationship. Following Freud, the baby was seen for a long time as a substitute for the woman's missing penis (Deutsch, 1945; Zilboorg, 1929, 1931). As a consequence of seeing the female as an "homme manqué", a castrated male, disturbances were often interpreted as being caused by frustrated phallic Oedipal strivings in women. As Chasseguet-Smirgel (1985) has so aptly pointed out, phallic sexual monism, as adopted by psychoanalysis, belongs to the vision of the male fetishist.

Post-natal depression doesn't figure in the index of the Standard Edition of the Complete Psychological Works of Sigmund Freud. As a consequence of Freud's theoretical and clinical inclination, mothers and maternity have long been neglected. Post-natal depression has seldom been elaborated theoretically or illustrated clinically, either before or after Blum remarked on this state of affairs in his 1978 paper. Infant research has provided new evidence about the devastating influence that the mother's depressed mood has on the baby (Brazelton, 1983; Cramer, 1983; Field et al., 1985, 1988; Lebovici, 1983; Soulé, 1983). Psychoanalysis traditionally considers mothers from the vantage point of the child, avoiding the question: What does a mother want?

The female dyad that a woman forms with her mother can lead, through several phases in her life and over several generations, to suppress aggression and obliterate differences. The mother–daughter symbiosis can remain unresolved throughout the life of a woman. In fact, the so-called normal symbiotic phase of development does not exist as such, as there is no phase in which the mother needs her child as it needs her. The dependence is normally one-sided, not mutual. But in some cases a narcissistically vulnerable mother needs her child more than the child needs her. Symbiosis becomes a euphemism for pathology: if the child is needed for the satisfaction of her mother's wishes, and the father is not functioning as the third person, the mutual dependency creates an unwholesome dyad. The normal Oedipal rivalry with the mother is suppressed. The father's role as in-between is important here. His emotional or physical absence or exclusion risks perpetuating a symbiosis in mother and child. The clinging within the mother-child couple demands the banning of aggression from the dyad. In this parasitic relationship, the child has to serve the needs of her mother in order to survive psychically, and both parties in this bond have to evade or suppress anger and hostility for the sake of continuing a peaceful symbiosis. Thus an illusion of mutuality is created, differences are obliterated, there is a pervasive assumption that they both share the same feelings and thoughts, and this is never challenged. The false idyll between mother and child remains quasi-intact at the cost of much psychic pain, as the dependent daughter suffers diminished self-esteem and misses out on normal pubertal protest, a precondition for individuation and autonomy.

Post-natal depression is a multigenerational problem. The woman who lives with an unresolved imaginary bond with her mother tends to repeat this problem with her child. She recreates symbiosis as an illusion, which can easily become a delusion. If the child complies with the mother's unconscious needs, the child's autonomy and her future successful motherhood are in jeopardy. This process tends to repeat itself over the generations.

Emotional involvement of women with their mothers and grandmothers facilitates transgenerational transmission of trauma. I reasoned that a symbiotic phase does not exist as such, as there is normally no phase in which the mother needs her child as it needs her. Some narcissistically vulnerable mothers need their child more than the child needs her. Symbiosis becomes a euphemism for pathology: if the child is needed for the satisfaction of her mother's wishes, without the father functioning as the third person, the mutual dependency creates an unwholesome dyad.

Multigenerational involvement in pathology means that more than one generation is involved in a serious emotional disturbance. As in the case of Ernestine, familial mythology and fantasies explaining traumas and disasters in the past, resulted in magical thinking, confusion, and shared delusions. Unconscious conflicts are more easily transmitted along the straight female line of descent, as matrilineal identification is not diluted by sexual difference.

Although problems in relation to the woman's mother have been noted by most authors on post-natal depression, whether the authors are psychiatrists or psychoanalysts (Bieber & Bieber, 1978; Douglas, 1963; Hayman, 1962; Jones, 1942; Ketai & Brandwin, 1979; Lomas, 1960a, 1960b; Molinski, 1972; Pines, 1972; Roth, 1975), the multigenerational links have received scant attention.

If treatment is successful, which is often the case in this period of rapid changes, Oedipal feelings will get a renewed chance to develop. Having a baby is, like adolescence, another chance to prove that a woman's anatomy is far from being her destiny.

It seems that, in women, only a partial separation from the maternal object has to take place. There is a very fine line between healthy relatedness and pathological symbiosis, as becoming a mother involves the ability to internalise one's mother as a caregiver. Only if sufficient triangulation has taken place does the Oedipal constellation have a chance in the puerperium. Women who have not resolved their relationship to their primary object remain in a vulnerable state and risk becoming depressed in the process of becoming a mother.

To prevent the consequences for the next generation(s), treatment of post-natal depression is indispensable and can be very effective if provided promptly. The emotional upheaval of a woman in the post-natal period gives her a better chance to restructure her psyche than at other times of her life.

References

Anthony, E. J. (1983). An overview of the effects of maternal depression on the infant and child. In: H. L. Morrison (Ed.), *Children of Depressed Parents* (pp. 1–16). New York: Grune & Stratton.

Asch, S. S. (1966). Depression: Three clinical variations. *Psychoanalytic Study of the Child*, 21: 150–171.

Asch, S. S. & Rubin, L. J. (1974). Postpartum reactions: Some unrecognized variations. *American Journal of Psychiatry*, 131: 870–874.

Benedek, T. (1973). The psychosomatic implications of the primary unit: Mother–child. In: *Psychoanalytic Investigations: Selected Papers* (pp. 255–276). New York: Quadrangle.

Bergler, E. (1959). Psychoprophylaxis of postpartum depression. *Postgraduate Medicine*, 25, 164–168.

Bieber, I. & Bieber, T. B. (1978). Postpartum reactions in men and women. *Journal of the American Academy of Psychoanalysis and Dynamic Psychiatry*, 6: 511–519.

Blum, H. P. (1978). Reconstruction in a Case of Postpartum Depression. *Psychoanalytic Study of the Child*, 33: 335–362.

Brazelton, T. B. (1983). Le bébé partenaire dans l'interaction [The baby as partner in the interaction]. In: M. Soulé (Ed.), *La dynamique du nourisson, ou quoi de neuf bébé?* (pp. 11–27). Paris: Les Editions ESF.

Brody, S. (1982). Psychoanalytic theories of infant development and its disturbances: A critical evaluation. *Psychoanalytic Quarterly*, 51: 526–597.

Chasseguet-Smirgel, J. (1985). *Creativity and Perversion*. London: Free Association.

Cramer, B. (1983). La psychiatrie du bébé [Infant psychiatry]. In: M. Soulé (Ed.), *La dynamique du nourisson, ou quoi de neuf bébé?* (pp. 28–83). Paris: Les Editions ESF.

Deutsch, H. (1945). *The Psychology of Women (Vol. 2)*. New York: Grune & Stratton.

Douglas, G. (1963). Puerperal depression and excessive compliance with the mother. *British Journal of Medical. Psychology*, 36: 271–278.

Field, T., Healy, B., Goldstein, S., et al. (1988). Infants of depressed mothers show "depressed" behaviour even with non-depressed adults. *Child Development*, 59: 1569–1579.

Field, T., Sandberg, D., Garcia, R., Vega-Lahr, R., Goldstein, S., & Guy, L. (1985). Pregnancy problems, postpartum depression, and early mother–infant interactions. *Developmental Psychology*, 21: 1152–1156.

Fraiberg, S. (Ed.). (1980). *Clinical Studies in Infant Mental Health: The First Year of Life*. New York: Basic Books.

Freud, H. (2011) *Electra vs Oedipus. The Drama of the Mother–Daughter Relationship*. London/NewYork: Routledge.

Gavin, N., Bradley, N., et al. (2005). Perinatal depression: a systematic review of prevalence and incidence. *Obstetrics and Gynaecology*, 106: 1071–1083.

Halberstadt-Freud, H. C. (1980). Proust and perversion: Some clinical and theoretical considerations. *International Journal of Psycho-Analysis, 61*: 403–410.

Halberstadt-Freud, H. C. (1989). Electra in bondage: On symbiosis and the symbiotic illusion between mother and daughter and the consequences for the Oedipus complex. *Free Associations, 17*: 58–89.

Halberstadt-Freud, H. C. (1991). *Freud, Proust, Perversion and Love*. London: Harcourt Brace.

Hayman, A. (1962). Some aspects of regression in non-psychotic puerperal depression. *British Journal of Medical Psychology, 35*: 135–145.

Jones, E. (1942). Psychology and childbirth. *Lancet, 1*: 695–696.

Ketai, R. M. & Brandwin, M. A. (1979). Childbirth-related psychosis and familial symbiotic conflict. *American Journal of Psychiatry, 136*: 190–193.

Khan, M. M. (1979). The role of polymorph-perverse body experiences and object-relations in ego-integration. In: C. Yorke (Ed.), *Alienation in Perversions* (pp. 31–55). London: Hogarth. (Original work published 1962)

Lebovici, S. (1983). *Le nourisson, la mére et le psychanalyste, les interactions précoces* [The infant, the mother and the psychoanalyst: Early interactions]. Paris: Paidos/le Centurion.

Lomas, P. (1960a). Defensive organization and puerperal breakdown. *British Journal of Medical Psychology, 33*: 61–66.

Lomas, P. (1960b). Dread of envy as an aetiological factor in puerperal breakdown. *British Journal of Medical Psychology, 33*: 105–112.

Mahler, M. S. (1968). *On Human Symbiosis and the Vicissitudes of Individuation: Vol. 7: Infantile Psychosis*. New York: International Universities Press.

McDougall, J. (1970). Homosexuality in women., In: *Female Sexuality. New Psychoanalytic Views*. London: Maresfield Library.

McDougall, J. (1986). Eve's reflection: On the homosexual components of female sexuality. In H. C. Meyers (Ed.), Between analyst and patient: New dimensions in countertransference and transference (pp. 213–228). Hillsdale, NJ: The Analytic Press.

Molinski, H. (1972). *Die unbewusste Angst vor dem Kinde: Als Ursache von Schwangerschaftsbeschwerden und Depressionen nach der Geburt, mit 12 anschliessenden Falldarstellungen* (The unconscious fear for the child: As cause of problems during pregnancy and depression after birth, with 12 pertinent case studies). München: Kindler.

Pines, D. (1972). Pregnancy and motherhood: Interaction between fantasy and reality. *British Journal of Medical Psychology, 45*: 333–343.

Pines, D. (1982). The relevance of early psychic development to pregnancy and abortion. *International Journal of Psycho-Analysis, 63*: 311–319.

Proust, M. (1981). *Remembrance of Things Past: Volume One. Swann's Way & Within a Budding Grove.* (Translated by C. K. Scott Moncrieff and Terence Kilmartin.) New York: Random House.

Roth, N. (1975). The mental content of puerperal psychosis. *American Journal of Psychotherapy, 29*: 204–211.

Soulé, M. (1983). L'enfant dans la tête, l'enfant imaginaire [The child in the mind, the imaginary child]. In: M. Soulé (Ed.), *La dynamique du nourisson, ou quoi de neuf bébé?* Paris: Les Editions ESF.

Stern, D. (1985). *The Interpersonal World of the Infant: A View from Psychoanalysis and Developmental Psychology.* New York: Basic Books.

Welldon, E. V. (1989). *Mother, Madonna, Whore?: The Idealization and Degradation of Motherhood.* London: Heinemann.

Winnicott, D. W. (1958). Primary maternal preoccupation. In: *Collected Papers* (pp. 300–306). London: Tavistock. (Original work published 1956)

Zachary, A. (1985). A new look at the vulnerability of puerperal mothers: A clinical study of two in-patient families at the Cassel Hospital. *Psychoanalytic Psychotherapy, 1*: 71–89.

Zilboorg, G. (1929). The dynamics of schizophrenic reactions related to pregnancy and childbirth. *American Journal of Psychiatry, 8*: 733–766.

Zilboorg, G. (1931). Depressive reactions related to parenthood. *American Journal of Psychiatry, 10*: 927–962.

CHAPTER FOUR

Parenting the next child in the shadow of death

Marguerite Reid

L ittle has been written about the experience of mothering or parenting a child when the new baby's birth follows a previous perinatal death. It is a topic that many people do not wish to think about. For some parents however, this is their experience. The feelings that are stirred up when a new baby follows a previous loss are complex; there is obviously joy but for many parents memories associated with the loss are still raw and undigested. Instead of feelings of pleasure and delight associated with a welcomed pregnancy, parents often struggle with a number of fears and concerns that do not necessarily lessen following their new infant's birth. If there are other children in the family, they too have worries and anxieties about the new baby.

In this chapter I will focus on the experience of both parents when they lose a baby and the way they describe their feelings about the conception of their next infant. I will then describe the difficulties some mother's encounter during this pregnancy and following the birth. Although I am focusing on perinatal death,[1] some of the details I write about may be helpful to parents who have lost an older child. In the second part of the chapter I will consider the difficulties experienced by some children when their birth follows the death of a baby or child.

Cain & Cain (1964) used the term a "replacement child" to describe an infant who is consciously conceived by either one of the parents to replace another child who has died a short time before. Of course, some parents do rush into another pregnancy following the loss of a baby and replacement baby dynamics are thought to be associated with unresolved mourning, denial of loss, and an early conception following a maternal bereavement (Leon, 1990).

Clinical work, however, with parents but in particular with mothers, has highlighted for me the complexity of feelings associated with the conception and birth of the next baby following a perinatal loss. I have found little evidence to show that mothers wish to replace, on a conscious or unconscious level; they simply wish to parent the baby they have lost. In fact, what has become increasingly clear to me is that mothers feel that they can never replace the lost baby and that they know they have to accept this on some level if they are to recover emotionally. My own sense is that the next baby is born in the shadow of the lost infant and therefore I prefer the term "penumbra baby" (Reid, 2007a). The definition of the term "penumbra" is a partial or lighter shadow round the perfect or darker shadow of an eclipse.

It is only during the last forty years that there has been any significant professional awareness of the distress caused to parents by the loss of a baby. The mythology attached to infant mortality in the past was that it was part of the pattern of life and death and the level of distress associated with it was not acknowledged. It was as though no one observed the grief of the mother or parental couple. The belief held by many was that a new baby would ameliorate the painful feelings associated with the loss (Reid, 2007b). Sadly, the reality was usually very different.

From a historical perspective, it is worth noting that Bourne (1968) carried out research in England that indicated that family doctors showed reluctance to know or remember anything about a patient who had suffered a stillbirth. He wrote that he thought a stillbirth was often perceived as a "non-event" that could not be categorised within a conception of illness. Similarly, in 1979, Lewis wrote that although a stillbirth is a tragedy that occurs in about one in one hundred deliveries, after a stillbirth everyone behaves as though nothing has happened. The bereaved woman is usually isolated, avoided, and then discharged as quickly as possible (Lewis, 1979). However, Cullberg (1971) commented on the prescription of heavy sedatives to women following the loss of a baby, as though there was professional awareness of the mother's distress. Slightly later, in 1983, Lovell considered hospital practice following a perinatal loss and she concluded that there seemed to be "… no physical or psychological space for a maternity case without a baby. Is she a mother or is she a patient?" (Lovell, 1983, p. 755). At this time, women were not encouraged to name, see, or hold their baby and the importance of a funeral or blessing was not acknowledged.

Fortunately, following this research there have been changes in hospital practice aimed at helping parents to feel that both they and their baby have been treated with dignity. They are encouraged, if they wish, to name and hold their baby and they are given artefacts such as footprints and photographs. Many parents desire a funeral or a service of blessing and others mark the loss by planting a tree or marking a place in a way that feels significant to them. It is hoped that by enabling parents to make decisions that feel acceptable to them at this time, that they will feel looked after and supported by professionals involved with their care and that this will help to facilitate the grieving process.

Despite the implementation of better hospital practice, what cannot be avoided are the feelings of trauma and distress when a baby dies. What is often not realised is the length of time that women and couples need to mourn when they have lost a baby. Much of my work is about enabling those bereaved by perinatal death to feel that they are allowed space within the consulting room and the therapeutic relationship to grieve; that they are not expected to carry on as though nothing has happened. I prefer to see women or parents following the loss, but often they are not referred until they have conceived again or have given birth to their next infant and are struggling with a myriad of complex feeling.

At this time, it is important to remember that when there are other children in the family it is often difficult for them to make sense of what has happened. Crehan (1999, 2004) wrote of the distress experienced by children when a sibling dies. This includes a new baby who they have not had an opportunity to meet. They can feel grief and guilt as well as ambivalence and they may find it difficult to express their feelings to their parents. Following a perinatal loss many children will try to protect their parents from further painful feelings by behaving as though they are all right. This can mean that little children are not given the help and understanding that they badly need when something as confusing as a perinatal death occurs. It is difficult for adults to make sense of what has happened and even more so for a young child.

I should like to describe some clinical work with a mother who was referred for psychological help some months after she lost her baby. This gave her an opportunity to think about the distress she felt following the loss and her fears about another pregnancy. Subsequently, I saw the couple together, and the space this gave allowed them to talk about the difficulties they were experiencing within their relationship following the loss, and enabled the father to talk about his feelings of grief. I think this clinical work clearly shows the level of distress experienced by parents and the complexity of feelings attached to thoughts about another pregnancy.

Lorna and Ben

Lorna's obstetrician referred her for psychological help eleven months after she had lost her baby. He described the baby as a much wanted pregnancy. Lorna and her husband Ben had met in their late thirties and both were soon aware that they wished to be together and to have children. They were equally aware that Lorna's age meant they should not delay a conception. Lorna conceived easily and both were thrilled when their regular scans showed the baby was developing well. A few weeks before the expected date of delivery Lorna woke with pain that she immediately thought indicated she had gone into labour. They rang their obstetrician who said they should come in to hospital. By the time they arrived, Lorna's labour was well-established but when the obstetrician tried to listen to the baby's heart rate he realised that the baby had died and that this was the reason for the baby's early arrival. The baby, a little girl, was named Bianca after Lorna's grandmother, who had died a few years earlier.

The referral for psychological help was made at a time when Ben wanted them to try to conceive another baby but Lorna knew she still felt overwhelmed by her baby's death. When I telephoned the couple I spoke to Lorna and she said she would like to see me on her own initially but that perhaps her husband could attend an appointment with her later. I agreed that I thought this would be helpful.

Lorna began her first session by speaking about her husband Ben's readiness to have another baby whereas she said she felt too frightened. Lorna sobbed as she described her delight when she discovered she was pregnant and she contrasted this happiness with the terrible feelings of grief and distress following the loss of her daughter. We thought of the shock she had felt when she realised she was in labour and she said that although her husband was quite optimistic when she went into labour, she was worried that something was wrong. The atmosphere in the room was raw with grief as she spoke of her disbelief that the baby had died; she had felt so attached to her from very early in the pregnancy. She was so looking forward to giving birth and caring for the baby. She wanted them to be a family, they both wanted to be parents so much. She told me that Ben had been very upset, he was longing for a baby too and she knew he felt terribly disappointed that she was not ready to think about another baby.

Lorna told me that the doctors had said the baby was perfect and they could not really explain why she had died. In a way, she said, that made things worse. If there had been a reason, she could have thought the baby died because she was ill; instead she was left thinking it was all her fault. She sobbed as she said she had not been able to take care of the baby; she had not been a good enough mother. She told me that it had completely rocked her sense of femininity, she no longer felt like a proper woman. Every time she left the house she saw mothers and babies and she just kept thinking it was so unfair, why was her baby not here? She told me that she felt so sad. I said I thought she still felt very shocked and traumatised by what had happened; there she was, excited about becoming a mother and suddenly she found herself without the baby she was longing to care for and love.

Lorna agreed, before going on to say that she had been working very hard at the time, trying to get everything sorted out before the baby's arrival. Perhaps she had not let herself rest enough. She said she had always loved her job and it was only when she met Ben that she realised she wanted to have a child. Until that point she had not really thought much about having children. Now, here she was in her late thirties, knowing if she did not conceive soon it would be too late, and yet she kept thinking about baby Bianca and how she had not been able to look after her. I said that Bianca was the baby she felt she really wanted to care for, not another, and of course you could not simply replace one baby with another. She agreed and said that she was her mother's first child and it felt awful that it was her first baby she had lost. I spoke about the way parents can develop a special attachment to the baby that is the same position as they were in their family of origin.

Lorna said there was a part of her that felt it would be disloyal to have another baby when she had not been able to keep baby Bianca alive. I asked if she thought the baby would be cross if she conceived again. She smiled and said the baby was so lovely, so perfect, and went on to describe holding her after the delivery, before saying that she did not think the baby would be cross.

We had several appointments to focus on Lorna's feelings about the loss of the baby. This enabled her to have space within the clinical session to think about her grief and how the loss had affected her. She then thought it would be helpful if her husband Ben joined us. This gave me an opportunity to think with the couple about their experience.

It had seemed from Lorna's description that they were at two different places in the mourning process. This easily leads to difficulties in the couple's relationship. My impression was that Ben thought he was ready to think about another pregnancy whereas Lorna still felt traumatised and shocked by the loss.

I was, however, aware that the referral had been made close to the anniversary of the loss. Anniversaries bring increased feelings of emotion and couples often find it difficult to support one another at such times. In their appointment together it became clear that Ben did not wish to pressurise his wife into another pregnancy before she was ready to conceive but instead he was feeling overwhelmed by Lorna's unhappiness. He wanted their marriage to be as it was, lively and dynamic, and he thought another pregnancy would give them a fresh start, a feeling of hopefulness. Lorna was so important to him he could not bear to see her feeling so unhappy.

Lorna looked relieved as her husband spoke, as though a burden was being lifted. We thought about the way feelings can become polarised between the couple. This can leave one member of the couple holding the feelings of sadness and grief, the other struggling to hold on to life and hopefulness. I spoke of the unbearable feelings that have to be contained in a relationship when a couple lose a baby. I explained that couples can mourn in different ways and it was important for them both to have an opportunity to talk about their feelings together. I stressed that they could each have a different experience of the mourning process, and so it was important that they had a space together to share their feelings.

Ben and Lorna then began to talk about how it was the anniversary of baby Bianca's expected date of delivery the following week; they were thinking they would like to mark the day in a special way. They had placed flowers on the baby's grave on the anniversary of her death a few weeks earlier but they thought they would like to visit one of their favourite places together and walk in the hills, just remembering her in a beautiful place.

This led to Ben describing the loss for the first time and how it had affected him. He spoke of his sense of shock, his initial belief that everything would be all right but then the realisation that their baby had died. He broke down and wept as he spoke of the beauty of the baby and agreed when I asked if he knew by looking at the baby that she was his daughter. Just as Lorna had spoken of not being a good enough mother, Ben now spoke of feeling he had not been a good enough husband; that he had not taken sufficient care of Lorna and this had led to the baby's death. Lorna immediately disagreed, saying he had been wonderful during the pregnancy, she had never thought him uncaring. It had been a lovely time.

Cudmore and Judd (2001, p. 153) stress the need, following the loss of a baby, for each member of the couple to act as a "psychological container or a secure base" for his or her partner, so that within this containing experience each partner might be helped to work through his or her grief. The closeness of the anniversary of the baby's death had, I thought, increased this couple's feelings of distress and grief. Although initially they had been able to support one another, at this time they had lost their capacity to do so. As our work continued, I thought my role was to act as a container for the couple's relationship, enabling them to explore their feelings without one being left with a sense of burdening the other.

It is useful to remember that a pregnancy has a natural time span from conception to birth. When a loss occurs during a pregnancy the expected date of delivery remains a significant time for the couple just as the anniversary of the death is clearly remembered. I think it is helpful if both dates are passed before a further conception takes place, as before this there can be a greater risk of the two babies becoming confused in the minds of the parents. Ideally, parents are encouraged to wait a year following a late miscarriage or stillbirth so that they have an opportunity to mourn prior to a further conception (Hughes, Turton & Evans, 1999).

A few weeks later, Lorna and Ben announced that they thought they were ready to think about another baby and, fortunately, Lorna again conceived quickly. There is a consensus in the research literature that a pregnancy following a loss is invested with special significance and that there is often an atmosphere of vigilance and anxiety (Phipps, 1985: Raphael-Leff, 1991).

I continued to support the couple during their pregnancy, something they valued, as they described it as a time of "mixed emotions". Quite soon after the conception, Lorna told me she had visited baby Bianca's grave to tell her that there was going to be a new baby. On some days the couple felt positive that all would be well but much of the time Lorna, in particular, was worried that she would not take the baby to full term. They had excellent obstetric care, with regular scans, and their obstetrician clearly held in mind the point in Lorna's pregnancy when she had lost her first baby. It was wonderful to receive the joyous message that Ben left, saying their new baby, another little girl, had been safely delivered by caesarean section that morning.

Lorna and Ben had an opportunity to work through some of their feelings of grief and distress before they gave birth to their next baby. Unfortunately, other parents do not have this opportunity and they are left struggling with complex emotions at this time. Family and friends often think that, following the birth, the parental couple will recover their emotional equilibrium, as they now have a healthy infant. This is not necessarily the couple's experience. The new baby can stir memories of the loss. The mother in particular is at risk of becoming depressed and, although there may be many loving feelings towards the new baby, on another level the mother can appear overwhelmed by the loss and persecuted by the new infant. She can find herself ruminating about the lost baby and this can lead to her becoming over-protective or negligent. Some mothers talk of having mistakenly called the new baby by the dead infant's name, as if concretely expressing their sense of confusion. When there is a difference in gender between the live and the dead baby some parents can feel regret and disappointment, which often leads to their feeling guilt that they cannot just welcome their new infant.

Much of my work at this time focuses on enabling mothers or parents to find a way to their new infant. This includes helping them to understand that many parents have feelings of confusion following the birth of the next baby and that this does not make them bad parents. When there are other children in the family they often feel worried that the new baby will not survive and this can lead to anxious protective behaviour or quite aggressive behaviour, as if testing the strength and resilience of their new sibling.

Falling in love is an important part of the relationship between the parental couple and their new infant. As we know, some parents immediately fall in love with their baby but for others it takes a little longer. Babies who are born following a perinatal loss are often in a vulnerable position. When the mother or the parents look at their new baby, it is difficult for them not to recall their hopes and expectations for the infant they have lost. It is as though the shadow of the dead baby comes between the parents and their live infant.

Many mothers who have shared their feelings with me at this time have talked of the pain associated with loving the new baby but of still feeling overwhelmed by memories of the loss. As a result the baby sees grief, distress, and sometimes anger in the mother's eyes, as well as feelings of love. I think this can lead to the new infant feeling confused and perhaps, on some primitive level, developing a sense of not being good enough. They are aware that there is another baby in mother's mind, a baby who takes her attention and means that she is not always emotionally available. Obviously there are always "others" in the mind of the mother but what the "penumbra baby" (Reid, 2007) often does not experience is the state of mind described by Winnicot as "maternal pre-occupation" (Winnicott, 1956). That is, that the baby is at the centre of mother's attention and that it is hard for her to think about anyone or anything else.

On another level, once parents have lost a baby it can be difficult for them to feel confident that they can keep the next infant alive. This can lead to the hypervigilance developed during pregnancy continuing after birth. Separation, feeding, and sleep can become major sources of anxiety. Some mothers describe finding it difficult to let anyone else look after the baby in case something dreadful happens. Sometimes this anxiety extends to the father and this can then cause problems in the couple's relationship.

Parents can feel worried about feeding their infant, ensuring they have enough nourishment to keep them alive. This can lead to anxiety about breast feeding, as it is difficult to measure the amount of milk taken from the breast in contrast to knowing how much milk the baby has taken from a bottle. If the mother stops breast feeding because of this anxiety, the baby loses the breast and all the good things associated with breast feeding, both emotionally and nutritionally. Similarly, when the baby is sleeping, mothers talk about worrying that the baby is dead and not just asleep. They describe anxiously checking, to reassure themselves that the baby is still breathing.

All these anxieties can lead to difficulties in the mother–infant relationship, often expressed by excessive crying on the part of the baby, refusal of food, or disturbances in sleep. As a result there can be worry about weight loss, or failure to thrive, or the baby wakes constantly during the night as if to reassure the parental couple that all is well.

For many parents these difficulties gradually lessen as they begin to feel more confident about parenting and, as a result, their infant flourishes. Mothers speak about their own mother being helpful at this time or their family doctor having encouraged them to feel more positive about themselves as parents. For others, however, their anxiety does not lessen but continues during their baby's first years of life. They worry about cot death and, for those who find separation difficult, the weaning process stirs considerable anxiety, as this symbolises separation from the mother. Most parents find anniversaries associated with the lost baby a painful time but for parents who are struggling to accept their new baby their infant's first birthday can be equally difficult. Often the "penumbra" baby's birthday falls close to an anniversary associated with the dead infant, which makes it even more difficult for parents to acknowledge feelings of sadness and, at the same time, celebrate new life.

I should like to use some clinical material from two mothers to illustrate some of these points. Both mothers encountered difficulties during the antenatal period as they tried to adjust to a pregnancy that followed a perinatal loss. The first mother, Claire, was referred during pregnancy and acknowledged that psychotherapy helped her to manage the distressing feelings she encountered at this time. Following the birth, she described the way our work had enabled her to turn to her new baby with strong feelings of love in a way that she could not have envisaged during the antenatal period. Nevertheless she agreed that complex emotions were stirred for her by the birth of the "penumbra baby", Daniel.

The second mother, Charlotte, was referred when her baby was six months of age. This pregnancy had followed a late miscarriage at twenty weeks. She was having difficulty relating to baby Hermione and felt considerable guilt about this. I thought she would have been helped by a referral for psychological help during her pregnancy, when she felt anxious and alone with her feelings of ambivalence. Her husband tried to help her with her complex feelings at this time but he was struggling with his own grief and anxiety.

Claire and baby Daniel

Claire was referred for psychological help when she was four months pregnant by her midwife who informed me that sadly Claire and Michael's first baby, a little girl, had died in utero shortly before her expected date of delivery. She said that Claire had waited two years before conceiving again but she felt extremely distressed now that her pregnancy was beginning to show. Claire decided to come to her first appointments without her partner, as she wished to have some space for herself. Michael joined the work later in the pregnancy and it was possible to work with the couple in a similar way to the clinical material described earlier in this chapter. I will focus on the difficulties that Claire brought to her sessions.

During our first appointment Claire spoke of dreading having to speak to colleagues about her pregnancy. Everyone would think she was thrilled and she was not. She felt so angry and said that if people commented "Now everything will be all right", she would probably completely lose her temper. I said that she seemed to be saying that she did not have space in her mind to contemplate a new baby whilst she was still grieving the loss of her little girl. Claire's midwife had told me that the couple had named their baby Sophia. Claire agreed and began to describe the feelings of hatred that she has to women who have a toddler who would have been Sophia's age. She said that a close friend was pregnant at the same time that she was and her baby is now two; it's awful, she told me, she just cannot visit their house. She exclaimed angrily, "Why should their baby be alive when mine is dead?"

I think it is important to stress that many women feel ambivalent towards their new pregnancy when a conception follows a perinatal loss. Claire had, sadly, declined a referral to the perinatal service following the death of her baby, as she might have found this helpful. It was, however, helpful that we had almost five months to think about her complex feelings before the delivery of the next baby. Most women who have suffered a perinatal death are terrified that they will lose their pregnancy or not give birth to a healthy baby and, despite Claire's feelings of ambivalence towards her pregnancy, these issues were raised during our work.

Claire had a well-managed delivery, close to term, and was encouraged to remain in hospital, supported by her partner, for several days following the birth. This enabled the neonatal team to monitor the baby's progress and both Claire and Michael received considerable support from the midwifery team in terms of caring for their baby and establishing breast feeding.

Fortunately, Claire fell in love with baby Daniel almost from the moment she saw him, and he flourished. I continued to see the couple with their new baby following the birth. He was a lovely baby, with a shock of dark hair, and he engaged with the world with considerable curiosity, something the parents delighted in.

I often observed that the baby engaged with me, initially through eye contact but later through moving close to me or handing me a toy, when the mother or parental couple spoke of baby Sophia. It was as though he knew that there was another baby in the minds of his parents and that I was there to help them all manage their feelings.

Charlotte and baby Hermione

The second mother, Charlotte, was referred for psychological help by her family doctor, when Charlotte's new baby Hermione was six months of age. She had lost a baby boy through a late miscarriage, twenty weeks into her pregnancy, and two years before the birth of Hermione. The baby who died would have been the couple's fourth child. The parents named him George after her husband's uncle. Charlotte now had three sons and one daughter.

I offered Charlotte an appointment on a weekly basis but it was often hard for her to attend. She missed many appointments and often came to sessions without baby Hermione. It was, however, noticeable that as her attachment to Hermione grew her mother brought her to more sessions. The session I should like to describe was Charlotte's sixth. Baby Hermione was almost a year old at the time and this session was close to Christmas.

Charlotte began the session by talking about a dream she had during the previous week and how she had found it upsetting. She once again talked about the miscarriage, as she had during previous sessions, this time telling me that following it she had cried for months, cried all the time, and then spent the next year thinking she should not be feeling this way.

She recalled going into premature labour after she developed a severe chest infection that was later diagnosed as pneumonia. She had not acknowledged how unwell she felt, she had just kept going, taking the boys to school and to their after-school activities. She spoke of her feelings of distress when she thought about giving birth at this time (twenty weeks gestation) knowing that the baby might have had a chance of survival if born just a few weeks later.

This led to Charlotte exploring her feelings about the birth of a daughter. She said she had always wanted boys and, although she was excited when she gave birth to her daughter, the excitement soon faded and she began to regret not having another little boy to mother. She spoke of how well Hermione fitted in with the boys, how it didn't really make much difference that she was a girl. I talked about the need to encourage the more feminine side of her daughter; she needed to know she was a little girl and that her femininity was valued. During a previous session we had talked about the way she felt her parents had not really encouraged *her* femininity. She smiled when I said this and acknowledged that her eldest son, Hamish, kept saying that Hermione was so beautiful she could be the fairy on top of their Christmas tree.

Charlotte went on to tell me she enjoyed taking Hermione out now, she no longer wished to leave her at home with the nanny as she had during her earliest months. When I commented that it was terribly difficult for mothers who had lost an infant to make space in their mind for another baby, she agreed, with a look of relief that indicated she felt understood.

When she came the following week she spoke of having thought about what we had talked about and she had bought Hermione a beautiful party frock to wear on Christmas Day. It was so pretty, it was a little girl's "dream dress" and she went on to say that her two older boys had said they could not wait for Christmas Day so they could see Hermione wearing it.

Although I had invited Charlotte and her husband to sessions, she wished to come on her own and did not wish her husband to be involved. Later she spoke of the difficulties they encountered as a couple following the loss but, as our work continued, she rediscovered her loving feelings towards him.

Following a perinatal loss I like to see either the parents or the mother with the new baby. Mothers often find it difficult to bring the "penumbra baby" to sessions, especially if they wish to describe more negative feelings. Charlotte was profoundly distressed following her late miscarriage, and physically unwell. She was aware that her other children had found it difficult to understand why the baby had died. She thought her third child had been quite severely affected, as he had begun to have nightmares at this time and had not wanted to go to nursery school. I thought it was as though his head was full of things he could not quite understand and that trying to make sense of them took a lot of his attention. I further thought that Charlotte would have found it difficult to be emotionally available to her other children following the loss.

Charlotte had always wanted sons; her late miscarriage was of a little boy and the subsequent birth of a daughter had raised strong feelings of ambivalence. This had contributed to her finding it difficult to mother baby Hermione. Eventually she delighted in having a daughter, as did her husband, but I thought her therapy had helped her to reach this point.

Mothers and parents can take a long time to recover from the loss of a baby or small child. Both Claire and Charlotte were still thinking about their dead baby and their individual experience of neonatal death and late miscarriage quite a considerable time after the loss. I think it is important to note that neither rushed into a subsequent pregnancy. Although they both had new babies this did not prevent them from yearning to mother their dead infant, although on another level they longed to fall in love with their new baby (Blackmore et al., 2011).

The child born in the shadow of loss

Meltzer (1988) stressed that the infant's emotional experience is one of the most important factors in the baby's development. Many of the mothers I work with during pregnancy and the post-partum period following a perinatal death, speak of feeling highly apprehensive and anxious during this time. I think this chronic level of apprehension can be conveyed to the baby, who then goes on to express this anxiety in muscular robustness and, subsequently, in overactive behaviour.

Mothers or parents who remain haunted by the loss of a previous infant can perhaps feel that they are caring for the wrong child and as a result "penumbra children" can develop a sense of feeling like the "cuckoo in the nest". As they begin to grow up these children often express anxiety that can be called "survivor guilt"; why are they alive when the baby is not? They can engage in quite risky life-threatening behaviour when they are in this state of mind. At other times they can feel triumphant that they are the ones who are alive. These children often think that they cannot be as important to their parents as the baby who died. This can be even more complicated when parents are at risk of idealising the dead infant, thinking they would have been perfect.

Some of the children that I see for individual child psychotherapy speak of feeling haunted by ghosts, and worried that the dead baby is angry with them for living with their mummy and daddy when they cannot. Others find it difficult to understand why the baby is not there and worry about burglars who steal babies. One little girl spent much of her time in therapy wanting to stick her favourite drawings to the inside of her therapy box, as she thought this was the only way to protect them from the burglar, who would take all her good things.

Children may idealise the dead baby. One little boy whose mother had not mourned the loss of a baby boy in a cot death eighteen months before his birth, told me his brother would have been a "great man", he would have been "the greatest man in my family". In my work with him there was always a sense that it was difficult for him to know who he was. He always thought that in order to please his mother he needed to be like the baby who had died.

There is usually rivalry between siblings but it is difficult to have a rival you cannot see. Children who follow a perinatal loss do not know how they would compare with the baby who died; they have no point of comparison. Of course, some parents manage this dilemma well by enabling the child to feel they were a much-longed-for baby. They are further able to help them with their feelings of rivalry and to encourage them to become individuals in their own right. For other parents it is more difficult and children can struggle with issues related to identification, or who they should be like, for many years.

I think Leon (1990) described this well when he wrote of the child's active participation in becoming a replacement, by wishing to relieve parental grief and secure parental love by modelling himself or herself on the image of the dead child.

Perinatal death leads to painful and complex feelings of grief. The impact on the parents, their existing children, and those born after the loss should not be underestimated. One of the mothers I worked with said that her stillbirth felt like a tornado which swept through her family, ripping it apart. Parents need space to mourn the loss, and hopefully this will enable them to make room for other babies, if they so wish. Some find support from family and friends or medical practitioners to be sufficient; others will benefit from a psychotherapeutic space to express the myriad of feelings stirred up by the loss of an infant.

References

Blackmore, E. R., Cote-Arsenault, D., Tang, W., Glover, V., Evans, J., Golding, J., & O'Connor, T. G. (2011). Previous prenatal loss as a predictor of perinatal depression and anxiety. *The British Journal of Psychiatry*, *198*: 373–378.

Bracken, M. B. (1984). Perinatal epidemiology. In: M. B. Bracken (Ed.), *Effective Care of the New Born*. Oxford: Oxford University Press.

Bourne, S. (1968). The psychological effects of stillbirth on women and their doctor. *Journal of Royal College of General Practitioners*, *16*: 103–112.

Cain, A. & Cain, B. (1964). On replacing a child. *Journal of the American Academy of Child Psychiatry*, *3*: 443–456.

Crehan, G. (1999). The Surviving Sibling: An Exploration of the Effects of Sibling Death in Childhood. Unpublished MA dissertation, City University, London.

Crehan, G. (2004). The surviving sibling: the effects of sibling death in childhood. *Psychoanalytic Psychotherapy*, *18*: 202–219.

Cudmore, L. & Judd, D. (2001). Traumatic loss and the couple. In: C. S. Clulow (Ed.), *Adult Attachment and Couple Psychotherapy*. London and Philadelphia: Brunner Routledge.

Cullberg, J. (1971). Mental reactions of women to perinatal death. In: N. Morris (Ed.), *Psychosomatic Medicine in Obstetrics and Gynaecology*, 3rd *International Congress*. Basel: Karger, 1972.

Hughes, P. M., Turton, P., & Evans C. D. H. (1999). Stillbirth as a risk factor for depression and anxiety in the next pregnancy: Does time since loss make a difference? *British Medical Journal*, *318*: 1721–1724.

Johnson, M. P. & Puddifoot, J. E. (1998). Miscarriage: Is vividness of visual imagery a factor in grief reaction of the partner? *British Journal of Health Psychology*, *3*: 1–10.

Kirkley Best, E. & VanDevere, C. (1986). The hidden family grief: An overview of grief in the family following perinatal death. *International Journal of Family Psychiatry*, *7*: 419–437.

Kohner, N. (1993). The loss of a baby: parents' needs and professional practice after early loss. In: D. Dickensen & M. Johnson, M. (Eds.), *Death, Dying and Bereavement*. New York: Sage.

Leon, I. G. (1990). *When a Baby Dies*. New Haven, CT: Yale University Press.

Lewis, E. (1979). Mourning by the family after a stillbirth or neonatal death. *Archives of Disease in Childhood*, *54*: 303–306.

Lovell, A. (1983). Some questions of identity: late miscarriage, stillbirth and perinatal loss. *Social Science and Medicine*, *17*: 755–761.

Meltzer, D. (1988). *The Apprehension of Beauty*. Strath Tay: Clunie Press.

Phipps, S. (1985). The subsequent pregnancy after stillbirth: anticipatory parenthood in the face of uncertainty. *International Journal of Psychiatry in Medicine*, 15: 243–263.

Raphael-Leff, J. (1991). *The Psychological Processes of Childbearing*. London: Chapman and Hall.

Reid, M. (2007a). The loss of a baby and the birth of the next infant: The mother's experience. *Journal of Child Psychotherapy, 33*: 181–201.

Reid, M. (2007b). Grief in the mother's eyes: a search for identity. In: C. Bainbridge, S. Radstone, M. Rustin, & C. Yates (Eds.), *Culture and the Unconscious*. Basingstoke: Palgrave Macmillan.

Winnicott, D. W. (1956) Primary maternal pre-occupation. In: *Collected Papers* (pp. 300–305). London: Tavistock, 1958.

Note

1. In describing miscarriage, stillbirth and neonatal death, Kirkley Best and VanDevere (1986, p. 432) wrote: "There are three pregnancy losses that are generally referred to as perinatal deaths, although they are misnomers in the literature". Perinatal deaths, as defined by the World Health Organisation are "… all fetuses and infants who are delivered weighing at 500 gr, or if birth weight is unavailable, 22 weeks or crown-heel length of 25 cm" (Bracken, 1984).

   Kohner (1993), cited in Johnson and Puddifoot, (1998, p. 1) wrote, "In the United Kingdom the 1992 Stillbirth Act deems 'stillbirth' to have occurred when a foetus is expelled after the 24th week of pregnancy. Any loss prior to this is termed: 'miscarriage' as prior to this point a foetus is considered non-viable".

CHAPTER FIVE

"Opening shut doors"—the emotional impact of infertility and therapeutic issues

*Joan Raphael-Leff**

"You know", says my patient Melissa, after trying to conceive for almost a year, "for a long time it wasn't that important to me to have a child. In fact earlier in my life I positively didn't want one, but now the desire is so intense it takes my breath away. The world is full of other people's babies. I also took it for granted I could just become pregnant. But why am I being denied?! I'm not asking for something unreasonable—*incredible* yes, but not unreasonable ..."

This chapter addresses the emotional turmoil experienced if heterosexual partners repeatedly fail to become a mother and a father, when ready to do so.[1] Childbearing may indeed seem "incredible" yet the "reasonable" nature of the desire to be a parent (expressed by Melissa above) is echoed by the World Health Organization's charter recognising "the basic right of all couples and individuals to decide freely and responsibly the number, spacing and timing of their

*This chapter is an updated and much revised version of ideas that appeared in "Behind the shut door: a psychoanalytic perspective". In: D. Singer & M. Hunter (Eds.), *Premature Menopause—A Multidisciplinary Approach* (pp. 79–112). London: Whurr, 2000. Permission was granted by Wiley, the current publishers.

children". I will suggest that our sense of entitlement is embedded in a tacit assumption from early toddlerhood that we each have a natural capacity to make babies. Our "generative identity" in childhood and adolescence contributes to the emotional significance of infertility when it strikes in adulthood.

While emphasising that each person's subjective experience of pursuing a baby is very different, I bring examples and verbatim quotes to illustrate the profound impact it has when basic trust in one's generative potential is nullified. This is particularly poignant for people who feel passionately, as Melissa does, that the time for parenthood has come. The obstacles posed by subfertility prolong the transition, revealing in "slow motion" emotional vicissitudes that are hidden by natural conception. Psychoanalytic psychotherapy can be beneficial, by offering the necessary containment and a place to explore and work through some troubling issues reactivated during this crisis.

Patterns of reproduction in the twenty-first century

Early identification with parents, siblings, and others encourage us to take for granted that our life-cycle awaits unfurling—a trajectory of childhood, adolescence, adulthood, and beyond that, parenthood will follow if we so choose, perhaps even grandparenthood, too. But we live in a changed world. Alongside feminism, availability of efficient birth control has fostered greater self-determination in women. We now feel free to decide when to have a baby, with whom, how, and indeed, whether to do so at all.

Today, with female-based contraceptive methods, the "morning after" pill, and safe abortion, almost a fifth of Europeans choose *not* to reproduce, and this figure rises among educated women—some forty per cent of whom in Germany remain "childfree" by choice. Around the world, in societies as diverse as Armenia, Bulgaria, Greece, Hong Kong, Italy, Korea, Latvia, Russia, and Spain the current birth rate has fallen to around one child per woman.

Confident in our fertility and/or the power of technology, when an unplanned pregnancy does occur many westernised women resort to abortion, preferring to remain childless for now, to keep the family small. Some postpone having a baby until they feel emotionally, professionally, economically, and/or socially ready to do so (often as menopause approaches). As a consequence, the number of first-time mothers giving birth over the age of forty has almost doubled in ten years, reflecting this trend for women to delay motherhood until they have built up their careers. Nonetheless, many fail to become parents even with the help of donated eggs. Postmenopausal mothers comprise just two per cent of all live births. More than three million babies have been born using *in vitro* fertilisation and other assisted reproductive technologies (ART) since the world's first IVF baby was born in 1978. However, availability differs dramatically across countries,[2] and success rate varies among age groups, and even across fertility clinics in the same city.

Our illusion of control over reproduction convinces us that as soon as contraception ceases conception will occur according to plan. But sadly, readiness does not necessarily produce a baby. Subfertility is prevalent. Meanwhile, the arrival of each period makes a mockery of having used birth control for so long to avoid the very thing the couple now seek so avidly. And, ironically, today's increase in fertility problems is attributed not only to waning fertility of delayed childbearing, but to the iatrogenic effects of some forms of contraception. Also, to silent sexually transmitted infections, and in close to half of all heterosexual couples, to reduced quantity, quality, and motility of sperm (possibly due to environmental pollutants affecting male embryos or men).

The prolonged nature of the experience necessitates a couple's questioning and reaffirming their wish to conceive (rooted in many motivators, some less conscious than others):

- a wish to operationalise "generative identity"
- a need to recapture lost aspects of the (baby-) self or to flesh out a fantasy baby
- seeking a sense of value or "someone to love/love me"
- pressure to meet or refute internalised parental ascriptions
- a desire to rewrite history, to repair or renegotiate incomplete developmental tasks
- a desire to cultivate the family line and/or to cheat death.

The repeated cycles of hope followed by anguished disappointment tend to become more acute as time goes by. The preoccupation with bodily symptoms is reflected in dreams, with growing awareness that the potential reproductive powerhouse can no longer be taken for granted. Realisation that something must be wrong alters the person's familiar body-image. With each new failure, the corporeal self seems to have declared itself a separate entity—an unruly traitor refusing to grant the heartfelt desire. But prolonged failure to conceive reactivates doubt in one's wider capacities, too. A terrible sense of helplessness and impotent dependency may reactivate the childhood frustration of feeling anxious, in need of help and excluded:

> "In my dream it's dark", says Melissa. "I see nothing. I'm crying and there's this loud banging noise—then I realise it's *me*, pounding on the door of my parent's bedroom. I feel frightened. Had a nightmare and want to come in their bed. But despite my yelling, my mother and father can't hear me. Maybe they're asleep, or having sex ... Whatever. I feel left out, scared and angry—sobbing, calling, hammering on the shut door—but there's no reply ..."

Like many others who have difficulty joining the "club" of parents, Melissa is angry and despondent, feeling excluded, like an oedipal child, left out behind the shut parental door. Before inviting Melissa to tell us her own story, it is important to understand more about the powerful impact the inability to conceive has on our self-conception as fertile men or women.

Generative identity

It is estimated that around a quarter of Western couples discover they have a problem after a year of trying and failing to conceive. Eventually, at least one in six of these couples go on to see a specialist. Approaches to having a child and reactions to prolonged reproductive failure, vary even within the same couple. Desperate to have a baby, one partner may feel overwhelmed by sadness while the other seems prepared to accept childlessness. Some agree to leave conception to "fate" or even decide to give up on the idea of a baby altogether while others opt for investigations and, after more deliberation, fertility treatment. If that, too, continues to fail, partners may eventually decide to stop. They resign themselves to childlessness, or negotiate adoption or fostering together. Disillusioned with their lack of joint creativity, others, may decide to part feeling they can no longer co-operate. Such separation can also be an act of generosity, in order to allow the fertile partner to have a child with someone else. Some people move on, saddened but relatively unscathed. However, many are severely traumatised by the experience, feeling less of a man or a woman for failing miserably where most automatically succeed. I suggest that this range of responses reflects variations of "generative identity" as experienced at this particular point in their lives.

Contemporary psychoanalytic theorising hopes to rescue gender from being treated as a single entity embedded in binary definitions. To this end I have redefined previous constituents and added a fourth component of gender formation (Raphael-Leff, 1995, 2007):

- *Embodiment*—the psychic meaning of one's sense of maleness or femaleness (based on bodily experience and parental assignment, defined in the past as "core" gender identity (Stoller, 1985))
- *Gender representation*—relating to self-designations and gendered performance of *femininity or masculininty* (previously defined as "*gender* role" (cf. Person & Ovesy, 1983; Tyson & Tyson, 1990; Butler, 1990))
- *Erotic desire* (previously articulated as "sexual partner orientation" (O'Connor & Ryan, 1994))[3]
- *Generative identity*—a psychic construction of oneself as *a potential progenitor* (Raphael-Leff, 2007, 1997/2008).

Parents emphasise their baby's sex from birth, or even before (especially, since the advent of ultrasound and amniocentesis). The mother and father's feelings about their own bodies, their sexuality and ideas about femininity and masculinity, will affect the way their male or female baby will come to see her/him self. Thus, long before language, a sense of sexed embodiment becomes established, through a combination of conscious and unconscious parental ascriptions and handling and the baby's own bodily perceptions and identifications. Then, as words begin to replace gesture, through interaction with peers as well as with older people, the toddler's understanding of gendered subtleties grows with the conscious discovery of sexual difference and social expectations about what it means to behave like a little boy or girl.

I suggest that although a young child can name genitals or differentiate girls from boys, generative identity is acquired at a time when a toddler begins to *re-evaluate* sexual distinctions. Between eighteen to thirty-six months, the little child who had hitherto imagined she or he could be and do "everything" comes up against some reality restrictions:

of *sex* (I can only be one sex, not neither or both);
of *genesis* (I am not self-generated but made by two others);
of *generation* (adults have babies; children cannot);
of *generativity* (adult females give birth and may suckle; males impregnate).

These basic facts of life cause painful deflation of the toddler's sense of omnipotent indeterminancy and magical control over the world. Awareness of sexual difference increases the child's interest in genitalia, and differences between his/her own, other children's and adults'. The significance of possessing one specific genital dictates that the child renounce the previous bisexual over-inclusiveness (Fast, 1984), along with the previous sense of invincibility. Growing awareness of separateness also increases the child's anxieties about separation, with fears about losing the parents, their protection and love. Throughout the "terrible twos", the child tests his or her limits with tantrums and battles over autonomy, and, hopefully, bodily ownership and care is gradually transferred from parent to child, whose physical mastery increases with walking, then running, jumping, and skipping, and control over urine, feces, and appetites. Concerns about bodily intactness now arise, with anxieties about loss, attack, and failure (in the past defined as "castration" anxieties). But recognition of bodily restrictions often results in acute feelings of humiliation, jealousy of the parents' freedom to do as they please, and envy of the other sex who may seem to have a better deal.

In the child who grows up with two biological parents, generative identity also involves accepting that mother and father have not only a sexual union but a reproductive function from which the child is excluded.[4] During the course of these preoccupations, erotic desire may become heightened towards one parent, with rivalry towards the other, and desire to give or get a baby—until, comforted by the promise of a baby of his/her own, and a spouse outside the family, the child relinquishes ideas of the parent or sibling as future partner.

In other words, acquisition of generative identity entails acknowledging and mourning one's own limitations:

- being separate and only *one sex* (rather than neither or both)
- *pre*-potent (rather than omnipotent)
- only *half* of future procreative coupling (interdependent rather than autonomous).

Depending on emotional circumstances at this crucial time, the growing child may learn to accept these facts of life, or becomes inhibited by their pressure. Some children may try to disregard these restrictions or disavows their reality, becoming increasingly rebellious, defiant and engrossed in compulsive play, enacting issues of sex, birth, death, or superpower omnipotence. Others may become depressed and anxious, fervently relinquishing any traits of the other sex, and restricting themselves to a sex-stereotyped range of behaviours. Yet others find more productive ways of negotiating restrictions, transcending these imaginatively through inventive play, reading, and expansion of their own creativity (Raphael-Leff, 2010b). Depending on parental reactions, their cross-dressing and interest in toys designated for the other sex, may be treated as a perverse refusal of the assigned gender or as playful, an act of broad-minded liberation.

I suggest that disturbances in generative identity are likely to arise in cases of inflexible or intrusive, humiliating parents, who are insensitive to the child's need for gradual "disillusionment". Or else in cases where traumatic life events (such as the shocking birth or death of a sibling, domestic violence, sexual abuse, forced migration, etc) coincide with this critical early period when the child is demarcating his or her generative potentialities. The actual reality of painful events at a time when imagination is still being disentangled from fact may lead to self-blame, and the child treating the trauma as the magical materialisation of his/her own thoughts, thus interfering with ideas of causality (Raphael-Leff, 2013).

However, when resilience accompanies generative identity, several momentous conceptual shifts become possible:

- the child changes from being someone else's creature or creation to becoming a potential (pro)creator in his or her own right;
- a shift may occur from emphasis on physical procreativity of a baby to an abstract notion of creativity in general;
- recognition that mental capacities are not sex-coded—the child may realistically recoup his/her cross-gender capacities, and achieve psychic liberation from the restrictive biological determinism of sex.

When all these shifts take place sanctioned by family and society, the growing child develops a sense of *agency*, feeling that irrespective of bodily sex and deferment of reproduction, she or he can make vital choices that influence the course of his or her own life. Indeed, in the West, largely due to feminist influences, children are increasingly encouraged to draw on their identification with attributes of *both* sexes, encompassing a variety of mental capacities and characteristics no longer restricted to stereotypical "feminine" or "masculine" categories of appearance, clothes, toys, sports, sex-typed skills (cooking, home-making or child-care) or "macho" behaviour. With educational parity, women can now participate more fully in the socio-economic and political life of their society, albeit still not with equal pay. Many come to realise that their generativity can be expressed in a variety of non-reproductive ways rather than having to wait for a baby to fulfil it. Growing up, such a person may come to experience gratification from the creative expression of a wider range of inner potentialities, and indeed, as noted above, some feel so fulfilled in work and social relationships that they experience little need to embark on parenthood. At a later stage some, like Melissa, find a beloved mate with whom they wish to reproduce. Or change their view due to other circumstances.

Back to Melissa

After many months of trying to conceive naturally, Melissa and her partner have begun extensive fertility investigations with inconclusive results. Increasingly, she feels they are living out a prolonged "nightmare", emotionally ready for a baby who never materialises. As her dream above indicates, rage intensifies as she feels "left out, scared and angry", excluded from becoming a parent. In her daily life, she suffers headaches, feels on the verge of tears all the time, and finds it difficult to concentrate at work. Her sleep is disturbed by vivid dreams. She often wakes bathed in sweat, feeling anxious and experiencing palpitations. For almost a year now, as each menstrual cycle has drawn to its close, she and her partner have eagerly sought signs of conception, especially when her period has been late, but sadly all the home-pregnancy tests have been negative. In recent months confusion has increased, as her cycles have become irregular with spotting rather than periodic bleeding. She is unable to tell whether these physical symptoms are the cause of her failure to conceive or are caused by her increasing unhappiness. Her partner feels equally distressed and frustrated by their prolonged malfunction and now he too is implicated, as his sperm count is found to be low.

Thirty-two-year-old Melissa had originally sought therapy with me shortly after marrying, saying she wanted to use twice-weekly therapy to explore the troubled relationship with her possessive mother in order to prevent problems when she herself becomes a mother. However, during the course of the year, while inexplicably unable to conceive, her perspective has changed and Melissa despairingly feels that if she cannot become a mother at all, nothing in her life will ever be right again.

Paradoxically, during the months of fertility investigations, the enigmas of reproductive sex are both heightened and dispelled with the incursion of the medical profession into the intimacy of their bedroom. Lovemaking is disrupted by their greater self-consciousness and the intensified scrutiny of physiological processes. Bodily configurations feel mechanised, and her body is rudely invaded by endoscopic and sonographic observations (that familiarise fertility patients with hitherto unknown internal aspects of their bodies, such as the silent growth of individual follicles or the thickness of the womb-lining).

After a prolonged spate of investigations, the defining moment of diagnosis eventually arrives:

> "I can't bear it", cries Melissa some days after being told she is suffering from premature menopause. "I look around me and there's a whole world I can't get in to. No fairness! *Why me?* At first I felt like shouting at everyone: "If you can why can't *I?* I don't deserve another struggle!' It feels like an unjust punishment but there's no-one to appeal to, and no-one to blame ... there's no rage any more, just helpless *weeping*—no point in even being angry with my body anymore, like before when I tried to coax it into working. I now know that whatever I do I can't *make* it happen!"

Fertility problems and psychotherapy

The current increase in fertility problems is almost equally distributed between men and women. Subfertility is partly a natural function of ageing due to postponement of childbearing, and partly attributable to environmental toxins, increased intake of medication, and the after-effects of a rising incidence of sexually transmitted infections. Only a very small proportion of cases of "unexplained infertility" may be attributable to psychological causes, and, with refined diagnostic techniques, this is decreasing. However, the majority of people do suffer from *the psychological impact* of infertility itself. Therapy can be beneficial during each phase, addressing the disturbing effects of trying and failing to conceive; the blow of infertility assessment and diagnosis; the unremitting and often painful demands of treatment procedures; and the outcome—how to accommodate to involuntary childlessness, or in some cases, to the challenges of parenthood after such a build up of hope, anxiety, and often unrealistic idealisation (Raphael-Leff, 2012).

The psychological impact of infertility

1. *Trying to conceive*: the dawning realisation that something is wrong often leads to embarrassment within the couple, and silent fantasies about what prevents them conceiving. Beginning to communicate may expose a divergence of priorities between them—one partner satisfied with the richness of their life as a couple, while the other rails against fate; one feeling desperately hurt and cheated, resigned to emptiness though aching for a child, while the other partner remains determined to get a baby at all costs. In this project they are *interdependent* and eventually must decide whether to seek help together, give up on the idea of having children, or find other creative solutions. Individual or couple psychotherapy enables them to explore why one is so despairing or treats this as a justified "punishment" for some previous "sin", or feels anxious about shameful social exposure or fearful of bodily intrusions during investigations. Talking therapies can help to resolve differences, enabling couples to decide whether they wish to live rewarding "childfree" lives together, or want to go ahead and find out why they have not conceived, and whether they can be medically assisted.

2. *Investigations* may be prolonged. Sometimes they involve physically painful, invasive, and humiliating procedures, including post-coital tests and reporting back to a third party about their private lovemaking. Studies have found that being scrutinised and monitored in routine hospital investigations increases the stress and tension and often induces sexual problems in the couple, which then necessitate counselling (Pengelly, Inglis, & Cudmore, 1995). Old feelings of disgrace and impotence come flooding back, as old attitudes towards the seemingly omnipotent parents of childhood are now transferred onto the fertile experts, who know how to "make" babies.

3. *Diagnosis* of infertility produces a further self-deprecating sense of feminine or masculine insufficiency. A man who unconsciously conflates virility and potency may feel mortified by his inadequate semen count or "sluggish" sperm, anxious that his partner may find him sexually inadequate and that others may regard him as less of a man. Similarly, a woman may feel shame at her "barrenness", seeing herself as failing in her "primordial feminine role". Both partners often experience humiliation at needing "help to do what any animal can".

4. *Treatment* brings yet another emotional "roller-coaster", with recurrent cycles of hope and despair, elation, and deflation. Beguiled by the promise that new treatments will transform their situation, many couples spend years having treatment, accommodating to ever more bizarre solutions—as the momentum of treatment cycles allows little pause for them to consider their personal needs. However, in therapy, there is a periodic chance to reassess the desire for parenthood, weighing up the emotional, physical, and financial toll of the predicament against the intensity of the wish to conceive.

For those who desire a baby, diagnosis of infertility need not condemn them to lifelong childlessness, as reproductive technology offers new hopes. However, the statistical reality is somewhat discouraging. There are very few egg-donors, the expensive treatments are beyond the reach of many, and the success rate is still very low. Only an average thirteen to thirty per cent of treatment cycles result in a "take-home baby". Sometimes, a family member or friend is recruited as an egg or sperm donor, but this new kinship category has emotional ramifications for all concerned. Adoption is another possibility, particularly for young couples, but few newborn babies are available in countries where unwed single motherhood is now socially acceptable, and even young teenage mothers choose to keep their babies.

As a result of treatment, some people do conceive and eventually have a baby. But as menopause no longer provides a cut-off point, many continue to pursue conception well into their forties or later, at great emotional, physical, and financial cost. Some do desist from treatment, allowing "fate" to take its course. Others resign themselves to childlessness, grieving their losses. They may even decide to take up contraception again, as an act of control, finding emotionally rewarding avenues outside of parenting. Yet others now invest their energies in pursuing fostering, or adoption of a baby at home or abroad. A proportion of people go on to seek new treatment solutions involving ever more complicated procedures, including receiving donated sperm, eggs or even mitochondria, a frozen fertilised embryo, or use of a surrogate. In these cases reproduction becomes a medically orchestrated procreational act, and people may become "fertility tourists", travelling to other countries on the European continent for eggs, to India or China for surrogacy, or South America, Africa or the Far East for adoptions, with long term psychosocial repercussions for offspring as well as parents.[5]

5. *Parenthood*: ART "success" is often measured by conception. People undergoing treatment focus on implantation and retention of the pregnancy. Becoming parents following prolonged infertility treatments may actually come as a surprise. Similarly, idealisation of the yearned-for elusive baby may result in disappointment at the ordinary one who arrives. Nonetheless, a study of IVF mothers rated them as highly attentive and the infants more playful (Papaligoura & Trevarthen, 2001), perhaps because of the emotional investment of producing these "precious" babies.

But the rapid switch of self-image and a very steep learning curve is fraught as people go directly from childlessness to baby care, possibly of (treatment-induced) twins or triplets and/or complications of prematurity. I suggest that due to the high anxieties and complex feelings along the way, in all cases provision of a therapeutic space for individuals or couples to think about the emotional consequences of their ordeal benefits all involved, especially as their own relationship is often compromised by the experience.

The impact on the couple

Reeling with disillusionment, a couple branded infertile may feel diminished by failure to fulfil the most fundamental prerequisite of the human race. Feeling singled out, they may isolate themselves in secrecy, overwhelmed by powerful emotions of envy, rage, sadness, and despair. Depression often centres on the existential crisis of being the last of a genealogical line. When a couple has been contemplating having a baby together, in addition to personal grief if only one them is diagnosed as infertile, she or he may feel guilt-ridden at depriving the partner of a child. They may also feel anger and resentment at the asymmetry of their positions, feeling cheated. If depressed or self-sacrificial, she or he may suggest separation to enable the other find a fertile mate, or may even become preoccupied with suicide.

Tensions often arise between the frustrated partners. Dissatisfaction with each other, and derision can fester below the surface or erupt in accusations. "I'll never forgive her if we've missed the boat" declares Simon. "I was ready for a child years ago but she kept putting it off saying we couldn't afford it yet". As their self-confidence plummets, self-blame and/or recriminations proliferate, with each partner grabbing at wild explanations such as illicit sexual encounters, previous terminations, or undue postponement of childbearing. Amicability may be maintained at a high cost of denied expression but the couple's relationship may further deteriorate as discrepant emotions are revealed.

Unlike Melissa and her partner, both equally invested in having a baby, Rachel's partner is happy for them to continue as a childless couple.

> "I feel so isolated. Alone with this *nightmare*", Rachel cries (using the same metaphor as did Melissa), following her diagnosis of tubal scarring: "I call it that because I don't want it to be happening, but I can't make it stop. I still find it hard to believe we can't make a baby together—but he doesn't seem all that bothered. Every morning I wake up again *into* the nightmare. In my dreams I am pregnant. In reality I am barren. It breaks my heart—but he says: 'What's for breakfast?'"

Helplessness in the face of uncontrollable reproductive processes infantilises, recalling those childhood heartaches of being unable to have babies like the adults. The diagnosis affects their love life, altering patterns of sexuality, sensuality, and psychosexual representations: "What's the point of having sex?" says Len. "It's tame stuff. Can't lead us anywhere". "I'm shooting blanks", says Charles, whose sperm count is minimal. These painful inner realities of deprivation, and the sense of incompetence and rejection, infiltrate night-dreams and daily activities with a sense of futility.

The couple's fertile friends may be avoided, as the world now divides starkly into "haves" and "have-nots". Unable to bear the sight and cooing sounds of contented new parents, many would-be mothers and fathers become socially isolated, in order to avoid engaging with people and their babies, even in the supermarket or park. Reeling between shock, denial, horror, rage, and sadness, they desperately try to find meaning in their own depleted lives.

In this emotionally laden atmosphere, magical thinking increases as an explanation is sought. Seeking meaning, they each scan the past for punishment-deserving misdemeanours, self-recriminations, and animosity towards the other. Subfertility may seem proof of destructive urges and/or forbidden desires, now revitalised. One noted female childhood anxiety is that damage to internal reproductive organs was caused by the (archaic) mother in retaliation for her little girl's envious fantasy-attacks (Klein, 1946). For some women, the situation of infertility retriggers such persecutory anxieties which resurface with a vengeance, cutting off possibilities of emotional contact with the mother or support from other maternal figures. At this junction, too, individual or couple therapy can help cope with the pain and facilitate a mourning process.

Feeling as powerless to force conception as they were in childhood, a couple in fertility treatment often experience themselves becoming infantilised by specialists, feeling once again excluded from "making babies" as they were from their mother and father's procreative relationship. Their rage may focus on their parents or on clinic staff who treat them paternalistically.

Even in cases like Melissa's, where reproduction has not been central to self-image, infertility can come as a great shock. Premature menopause betrays basic trust in time. When ovulation ceases, it abruptly ends the fertile years a woman had imagined stretching ahead of her, eggs ripening in monthly succession, one of which might have been fertilised when she felt absolutely ready to be a mother:

> I used to imagine my insides as this nice cosy place where the eggs all nestled waiting their turn", says Melissa. "Now it seems rotten in there. A dried up wasteland and the nice round full eggs are shrivelled, useless, empty duds [failures]. I'm a neuter! I can't even do what any bitch can. How can I feel feminine if I'm not even female anymore?!

Melissa has a long emotional journey to restore her previous identity as a richly endowed and multifaceted woman who is not reliant on egg production for a sense of her own creativity. Lifelong emotional difficulties with her competitive, judgmental, and possessive mother have to be worked through to (re)gain a sense of herself as an autonomous insightful person as well as a potential mother. Now that she feels ready to be a parent, further therapeutic work focuses on joys of interaction with a future baby which do not necessarily pivot on genetic connections but on her own capacity to give and receive love. Gradually, pleasure in her body's shape, its sensuality and its fitness replaces the bitter disappointment she has felt in not swelling with pregnancy. Melissa and her husband decide not to pursue gamete donation, and are accepted on an adoption list.

Gender identity

Many cultures still demarcate gender roles in stereotypically restricted ways. As noted, in some Western societies it is becoming acceptable for either of the sexes to demonstrate traits formerly reserved for the other. Females can now engage in assertive behaviour and pursue interests previously deemed unsuitable for "ladies", while men can be nurturing and emotionally sensitive in ways which were regarded as unmasculine or even effeminate. Indeed, some Scandinavian countries now offer equal parental leave for fathers.

I suggest that gender identity is not a fixed state. During adulthood our cumulative experience is recurrently reworked, leading at different times to reinterpretation of our subjective experience of facets of the bodily sense of fe/maleness, the changing meaning of our social roles and erotic desires, our sexual orientation and symbolic representations of generativity and fertility, feminine and masculine identifications, and maternal/paternal capacities—all within a fluid yet abiding sense of self. For each individual, accessibility to his or her own unique mix of internal resources depends on the degree to which personal gender identity is freed from strict male/female binary divisions, with entitlement to use his or her own "cross-sexed" capacities. Access to internal richness necessitates a tolerance of otherness, of difference, incongruity, contradictions, and ambiguity within the self. "Do I contradict myself?/ Very well then I contradict myself; (I am large, I contain multitudes)" (Whitman, 1855).

Generative identity and childbearing

This formulation helps us to answer the question of why some people are so devastated by their inability to conceive while others adjust, albeit with a sense of profound loss. I propose that in adulthood, infertility appears to hit hardest those who have unconsciously invested all their potential creativity in deferred procreativity (Raphael-Leff, 1997, 2002, 2010a).

Childhood recognition of the limitations of gender (only one sex), genesis (not autogenesis), generation (age-restrictions), and generativity (only half of a procreative union) can take different courses:

- acquiescence and promise of future reproduction
- denial of restrictions, leading to gender dysfunctions or omnipotence
- imaginative use of internal resources to overcome limitations and deferment.

However, our sense of self is never entirely stabilised and, given the right partnership or circumstances, a fierce desire for a child often arises even in those who have not dwelt on this previously. If, at this point, they are unable to produce a baby, the loss, while saddening, may not be experienced as devastating. The couple can go on to live a rich and fulfilled life. Although remaining childless themselves, they may embark on projects involving other people's children, or their own creativity.

Conversely, when the sense of generative identity has remained embedded in physical reproduction, having a child may feel like the long-awaited central goal of self-expression. A woman will feel herself "wiped out" by failing to become pregnant when she is ready to do so, if from early childhood her feminine identity has been embedded in pregnancy, taking for granted that when she grows up, like her mother, she too will create a baby with her own egg, in her own body. Despair sets in when the childhood promise of procreating a child of her own is broken. To such a person, diagnosis of infertility, whatever its cause, is devastating. When life has been put on hold, lived in unconscious anticipation of future childbearing as the culmination of female fulfilment, failure to conceive or to carry the baby to term signifies a major loss of femininity, as her identity collapses back into narrowly defined reproductive capacities. Similarly, a man who sees virility and/or genetic continuity as the defining theme in his life will feel annihilated and humiliated by the need for sperm-donation, and should it succeed, nursing the secret of his child's origins.

This was not the case with Melissa. During the course of therapy, as each partner painfully relinquished hope of a naturally conceived child of their own, they began to disentangle the pressures inherent in physically producing a genetically related child. Recognising their parenting capacities as distinct from reproductive ones, they began to envisage themselves as potentially loving and gifted parents to a child not-of-their-making. Thoughtfully working through their own early experiences, their empathic understanding of the other increased. Together they grieved the "special" baby they were unable to create, and the satisfaction of her belly ripening to give birth to *their* baby, as each of *them* had emerged from a mother's womb. Melissa felt she could now forgo the pregnancy and her partner his contribution to it, without feeling total failures or losing their respective positive self-image. And as they came to understand influences of their own family constellations and the unconscious dynamics that led to their fierce desire for a joint child, the couple decided that even if they could never reproduce together, they had much to give to a child in need of nurture. Rather than take the risky route of creating a baby through reproductive technology, they opted to care for an existing child.

IVF: sperm and ovum donation

Thus, infertile couples find different solutions to their plight. As noted, those who resolve to give up becoming parents may adjust with relative ease. Some accept involuntary childlessness most reluctantly, painfully acknowledging a diminishing yet ever-present sorrow. Depending on the diversity of their respective internal worlds, and their creative capacity to sublimate facets of their generative identity, many people eventually find ways to build on the fullness of their inner lives, tapping into alternatives that do not involve physical parenthood. Others decide to foster or adopt a child. Yet others decide to separate, amicably or in bitterness, finding their life together an intolerable reminder of their dashed hopes. Yet others feel unable to give up their burning desire for the conception which they feel will change their lives. They sign up to pursue increasingly complex and demanding medical treatments with varyings degrees of hope or desperation.

Donated eggs are used when a woman carries an inherited disorder or is unable to produce fertile eggs (due to menopause, genetic malformation, ovarian failure, or sterility following surgery or chemotherapy). A donor may have completed her own family or may be undergoing fertility treatment herself, with stimulation to produce multiple oocytes. These women are sometimes encouraged to share their surplus eggs to help other women or to donate them for research purposes.

When fertility treatment involves egg donation, complex conscious and unconscious factors can come into play. These affect the pregnant woman's connection with her foetus, but may influence implantation. Sometimes, even brief psychotherapy may resolve these issues.

Sarah, a thirty-seven–year-old woman with no previous interest in "deep" psychological understanding comes to consult me some years into fertility treatment with donated eggs:

"I have so much to be thankful for—my partner, friends, family, work. But my life has become consumed by this wish to have our … his … child. The more it doesn't happen, the more it becomes an issue. Years ago when we first got together I became pregnant but had an abortion as we both were young and wanted to travel. We had such a great time together, just the two of us. We went all over the world, always together. Even when we came back home, for some years having a baby was a far-off thought. We enjoyed our life as a couple, didn't really want an intruder into our twosome. Then in our thirties it seemed a baby would be a happy bonus in our long relationship—an anticipated gift-to-come.

"Now, after years of trying, there's a constant ache of something missing. Our *house* symbolises it: in the many years since we moved here I feel it acutely. This lovely big family house just waiting, empty. Time stands still. Most of the time, I do nothing. I'm scared I'll jinx it if I decorate a room for a baby. On the other hand, sometimes, I feel like rushing out to the shops and buying baby-clothes. Crazy idea but it feels like the only way to break this *suspended animation*.

"I suppose coming here to see you is another bit of magic. The doctors can't find a reason why these donated eggs don't implant—so it must be in my mind. At times it feels as if I've lost interest in everything—my work, friends, my life—I'm just despondent and waiting, always waiting … For a few months [after the diagnosis] it was terrible. I didn't feel like going out or seeing people … did nothing but cry. Felt it was unfair on my partner, tried to stop myself being so depressed, but the sadness is always there and sometimes I wonder if I feel if I'm miserable enough will this punishment be lifted?"

"Punishment?" I repeat. Sarah pauses thoughtfully, then interestingly, uses a similar metaphor to Melissa, of being excluded, behind a shut door: "I'm not sure why I said that. I guess when I was very young I felt punished when my mother left me on my own. I know she was busy with all the others and the housework as well, but I felt angry, left out—*punished*. I was the only one in the house who slept in a room by myself. They were *all in pairs*, my parents, my two older sisters and then when the little twins were born, they were always together, too. I used to creep down the hall and listen outside those shut bedroom doors—inside, each couple would be happy together, laughing or talking. And they *all had babies*—my sisters each looked after one twin; my mother and father had us; only *I* didn't have a baby. It's *still* true—they've all got children now. In fact, even my niece is pregnant. Only *I'm* still trying …"

"Funny, I remember when I was five and Dad told me Mum was expecting—it was like being *kicked in the stomach*. I still get that jolt when people tell me someone is pregnant—strange, goes right through me, as if madly jealous! Feels as if they're stealing *my* baby from me! I try to be rational but everything seems so meaningful these days. When I hear that someone conceived—rather than feeling: 'Good! That means we've got a chance too!' it seems as though if *they've* got the baby we can't have it … [long thoughtful silence] … I guess I still feel shut out … like that little girl standing forlornly behind those shut bedroom doors …"

At her initial interview we'd made an agreement to meet for six sessions during which this hitherto un-psychologically minded woman began to trace connections with past suppressed feelings—permitting herself to open "shut doors" in her mind. Gradually, as we explore less conscious aspects underpinning her hypersensitive sense of feeling an outsider to a couple, we realise that there is yet another couple from which she now feels excluded—the coupling of her husband's sperm and the donated egg. Not only was her partner "betraying" the adult-her with another woman to produce this baby, but the two little fertilised embryos in the lab Petri dish were also invested with powerful feelings from childhood when her mother betrayed her by joining forces with father to create the twins.

Finally, it also emerged that she was afraid of experiencing pregnancy, as the symptoms would remind her of having aborted her own first unwanted pregnancy. All the cost and effort to procure conception with a donor egg seemed a harsh rebuke—a severe payment, made by them both, for a baby they casually "threw away" in their teens, who today would have been as old as her pregnant niece. Two months after we ended our sessions she jubilantly phoned to tell me that she was pregnant.

When problematic issues remain unprocessed, an "adopted embryo" or baby born of donor sperm or egg, may continue to be regarded as "alien". If a couple has previously experienced a miscarriage, or has not grieved the loss of their own genetic baby, the baby, however fervently anticipated, may be seen as a poor "replacement", or one that does not rightfully belong in their family. Charged with intense ambivalence, and never feeling "right", the parents wish she or he was another.

In addition, there are practical and ethical dilemmas around gamete donation. Disclosure is becoming a very heated topic of debate, with some mental health professionals and parents arguing that every child needs to know his or her origins and should be told as early as possible. To them, withholding the information seems immoral, because family secrets can be devastating and/or because genetic histories are becoming increasingly important as scientists explore the hereditary aspects of disease. On the other hand, in the UK, now that donors have to be registered, there is a shortage of those willing to be identifiable. Some professionals believe that the parent's decision about disclosing assisted reproduction is a deeply personal one. Some parents fear their child will love them less, or that the grandparents will disapprove, or dread being stigmatised within their ethnic group or religious subculture. Therapy can help would-be parents with their own deliberations—which involve not only conscious considerations but unconscious factors too.

Early menopause

The loss of fertility before reproduction ends a person's direct genealogical lineage. Located at the *end*, rather than the middle, of a chain of inheritance, "falling off" the generative trajectory of all the preceding generations. While some people knowingly choose this position by deciding not to have children, it is particularly shocking for a young woman who has not yet fully contemplated the real choice of whether or not to have a baby:

> "My whole future is smashed", sobs nineteen-year-old Sophie, recently diagnosed with a metabolic condition which has led to

ovarian failure. "My friends chat on about discos they've been to and boys they've met, relationships, pregnancies, babies—but all those doors have been slammed in my face. I wish I was dead … No! I *am* dead—I'm dead before I have even lived", she wails inconsolably.

Not only does Sophie feel old before her time, but all her unrealised wishes, her nebulous hopes and dreams for "one day" are suddenly rendered obsolete; like Melissa, the potential of her eggs has evaporated long before their "best by" date. She feels bewildered in a topsy-turvy world in which she joins the older generation, struck down at the very time her adolescent peers are celebrating their newfound triumphal surge of potent sexuality. Sophie feels isolated, baffled, and betrayed; furious at no one and everyone, especially her mother who gave birth to a child with this genetic defect. How can anyone understand her plight—least of all her own mother who *has* been pregnant, has had a child and at forty-three may still be fertile?

In her late teens, long before the mid-age watershed of menopause, Sophie confronts her genetic extinction. It reverberates in her *cri de coeur*: "I *am* dead", as mortality looms, no longer refracted through a line of genetic continuity. On another level, seeking explanations, she wonders whether her bulimia has contributed to her condition and now sees her slim body as grotesque and mannequin-like—a celluloid doll with "no insides". She feels herself to be "a female freak and fraud", no longer a budding fertile woman but an "empty shell", devoid of femininity, creativity, generativity. With the blow to her generative identity it will take many months of therapeutic self-exploration to work through her anxiety, rage, envy, and profound sense of being cheated before she can accept that her value as a person is not diminished by her condition.

Compelling forces

As noted, some women renounce childbearing while others believe that pregnancy is a quintessential female right, which they cannot forgo, come what may. Faced with the prospect of a hysterectomy, twenty-eight-year-old Maria is determined to become pregnant as soon as possible. So much of her feminine identity is invested in reproductive generativity that she feels unable to contemplate life without having been pregnant. However, as a proud Catholic she is unwilling to enter a compromising heterosexual relationship for the sake of a baby. Wanting "the best", she investigates the possibility of procuring a "straw" of frozen semen from an American sperm bank advertising its sources as "Nobel-prize candidates". Some months of her precious time are dominated by these deliberations. In her therapy sessions she tries to engage me in the choice of the optimal "gene-father" for her baby ("The blue-eyed blonde engineer or the red-haired nuclear physicist?"). My interpretations that she seems to be wishing to replace her own absent father with an ideal fantasy one for her baby, fall on deaf ears. Gradually, through a dream of smothering a kitten, we begin to glimpse some unconscious roots of her compulsion to have a child to replace the baby her mother lost to cot-death when Maria was two years old. The dead baby was never mentioned again in the family and at times Maria believed she had imagined her existence. However, an aunt verifies her account and we begin to recognise how Maria's estrangement from her home country reflects the sense of futility of her lifelong desire to enliven and compensate her silently bereaved mother. Maria is driven by a sense of irrational guilt that she somehow "caused" her baby sister's death and her father's desertion. Gradually, as she accepts that rivalry and childish fantasies of getting rid of her sister did not magically cause the infant's disappearance, the burden of her imagined transgression lifts and her compassion gives way to anger. She is now flooded with rage at her depressed mother's emotional unavailability at the time, when she too was grieving the loss of the promised little companion. The toddler Maria was confused and frightened by her parents' inability to protect the baby from harm. Anger at her mother's rejection gives way to rage at her father, for leaving them both at such a difficult time. These internal changes enable Maria to now make contact with her estranged mother and to communicate with her in a way she felt unable to do while growing up. Consciously she wants to continue the "blood line" of her family, and to heal her own childhood scars by giving her baby the happy childhood she feels she missed.

Time is running out for Maria. Much remains unresolved in her therapy. However, faced with the prospect of the imminent hysterectomy she is determined to become pregnant as soon as possible. The surgeon agrees that her operation can be postponed for one year, and now that there is some flexibility, the loss of her uterus seems a medical necessity rather than yet another inflicted deprivation. Maria chooses to return to her country of origin and with her mother's help approaches a sperm bank of her own religious group, conceiving with the first insemination, carrying the baby to term, and bringing up her little girl in her mother's home.

This case illustrates the many unconscious fantasies that may be involved in a yearning to conceive, such as the desire to placate a depressed mother, to replace a dead sibling, to reproduce a childhood situation (of a fatherless child). The variety of parameters offered by assisted reproduction may reveal the desire to be pregnant and the wish to nurture. Faced with infertility, some couples feel they must have a genetic child of their own. Some acquiesce to childlessness despite the availability of technological resources or possibility of fostering, while others feel compelled to continue trying at all costs.

As noted, in my view these variations hinge on timing of events during the period of acquiring generative identity. In Maria's case, the sudden death of her baby sister during her own toddlerhood confronted her with an irrevocable disappearance that could not be rectified despite her desire for reparation. Furthermore, her bereaved mother's prolonged emotional withdrawal followed by her father leaving home for a mistress, seemed to further confirm little Maria's belief that she was not enough for her parents. Her conviction about the destructive power of her own intense emotions of love and hatred instigated a lifelong determination to produce a real *live* baby to reverse the tragic events of her early childhood.

Power of the past

On the basis of intensive treatment of some 150 people seen one to five times per week over the past thirty-five years in a psychoanalytic practice specialising in reproductive issues, I have found that the process of assuming generative agency is never completed. Reappraisals occur during transitional phases in the life cycle—puberty, menstrual periods, pregnancy, childbirth and lactation, or menopause when the distinction between female and male sexed bodies peaks unavoidably. Re-evaluations are also necessitated by traumatic life events such as pregnancy loss, severe illness, premature menopause, or hysterectomy. As I have suggested, the deleterious effect of these crucial events will be intensified by the degree to which personal identity has been invested in *physical* generativity (rather than its sublimation).

When, as in Maria's case, the trauma occurred during the critical period of the toddler's acquisition of her own generative identity, generativity itself seems fraught with dangers. This is especially so if there is little help in processing the original feelings. People who in their early childhood experienced unresolved and inexplicable happenings (e.g., maternal obstetric complications, perinatal death, parental infertility, prematurity, or even childhood sexual abuse) may operate relatively unproblematically until confronted once again with reproductive issues in adulthood. Clearly, to a person with this type of emotional psychohistory, an experience of miscarriage, stillbirth, subfertility, or premature menopause in their own lives is laden with psychic significance.

Clinical experience leads me to the idea that when such traumatic events coincide in time with the process of acquiring generative identity, unless the little child is helped to work through the emotional impact, she or he will unconsciously express the trauma through *concrete re-dramatisations* of past events in the present. Furthermore, the fact that the trauma occurred *in actuality* rather than fantasy propels the need to re-enact it in reality. The child, and later the adolescent or adult, will unconsciously go on attempting both to express the original trauma and to find compensation/reparation through such externalised realisation.

For some, unresolved anxieties may result in phobic avoidance of sexuality (another reason for delayed childbearing). Others may bypass the whole question of reproduction by opting for sterilisation, and/or other defensive psychological measures. Yet others show obsessional determination to control reproduction. Propelled by a blind need to disprove childish anxieties, some people manically dice with danger. Bravado over the internal generative conflict can be played out in external reality—in promiscuity, risky exposure to HIV or other infections, recurrent acts of conception to prove fertility followed by repeated abortions which enact conflicts between life and death, creativity and destructive forces, that seem inherent in reproduction.

These days enactment may be aided and abetted by use of reproductive technologies which enable our wildest fantasies to be lived out in reality—in seemingly self-generated babies, or driven acts of donating sperm or egg, realising powers both of generosity and of withholding. In extreme cases, the compulsion to express an unprocessed trauma may culminate in criminal acts of impulsive baby-stealing, sexual or violent child abuse, or even infanticide.

Enactment may also manifest bodily in psychosomatic ways such as psychogenic infertility (of psychological rather than physical origin), pseudo-cyesis ("pretend" pregnancy), or "couvade" in men who unconsciously mimic symptoms of pregnancy, miscarriage, or labour. Other disturbances in generative identity are expressed in rigid gender-polarised self-representation as "pure" feminine or macho-masculine. Finally, disturbances may also result in concrete thinking and an inhibited originality due to conflation of procreation and creativity. All these may benefit from psychoanalytic psychotherapy although they are not often self-referred.

Conclusion

Dealing with unexpected infertility is always a major life-event, whether it comes as the result of ageing, an ectopic pregnancy, surgical intervention, or biochemical causes. Being unable to reproduce when ready to do so compels a person to revaluate their generative identity. The man, woman, or couple are forced to reappraise their sense of self and expectations for the future, and explore the nature of the ideal family they had imagined themselves creating. Those who have hitherto chosen not to have children may remain relatively unaffected. Some opt for a genetically unrelated child to bypass issues of heredity. However, for people who historically suffered complications in their families of origin in their early years, or whose sense of generative identity has remained rooted in physical procreativity for whatever reason, the prospect of alternate solutions, be it creative sublimation, childlessness, adoption, fostering, surrogacy, or donated gametes, feels untenable as long as there is felt to be any glimmer of hope of a baby of their own.

Psychotherapeutic help during this critical period is essential. It offers an opportunity to work through some of the relational difficulties that infertility triggers between the partners and within each of them. Coming to terms with infertility, and mourning the genetic baby they cannot have enables them to greet the new baby as "new" rather than an ambivalently charged poor "replacement". By processing traumatic events from the past some people find the freedom to transform a sense of victimisation, and/or body-based system of generative identity into a sense of creative *agency*, that releases "multitudinous" facets of the self. In my clinical experience, this broader focus maximises receptivity to medical intervention and to the emotional issues involved. But it also helps cushion against hopelessness when pregnancy is not a viable option. We may say then that psychotherapy can promote a thoughtful capacity to unlock psychic "doors" within the self, rather than just anxiously pounding on the physical one which has slammed shut.

References

Butler, J. (1990). *Gender Trouble: Feminism and the Subversion of Identity.* New York: Routledge.

Fast, I. (1984). *Gender and Identity: A Differentiation Model.* Hillsdale, NJ: Analytic Press.

Klein, M. (1946). Notes on some schizoid mechanisms. In: *Envy and Gratitude and Other Writings 1946–1963.* London: Hogarth, 1984.

O'Connor, N., & Ryan, J. (1993). *Wild Desires & Mistaken Identities: Lesbianism and Psychoanalysis.* London: Virago.

Papaligoura, Z., & Trevarthen, C. (2001). Mother–infant communication can be enhanced after conception by in-vitro fertilisation. *Infant Mental Health Journal, 22*: 591.

Pengelly, P., Inglis, M., & Cudmore, L. (1995). Infertility: couples' experiences and the use of counselling in treatment centres. *Psychodynamic Counselling, 1*: 4.

Person, E., & Ovesey, L. (1983). Psychoanalytic theories of gender identity. *Journal of American Academy of Psychoanalysis, 11*: 203–226.

Raphael-Leff, J. (1995). Imaginative bodies of childbearing: visions and revisions. In: A. Erskine, & D. Judd (Eds.), *The Imaginative Body— Psychodynamic Therapy in Healthcare.* London: Whurr.

Raphael-Leff, J. (1997/2008). The casket and the key: thoughts on gender and generativity. In: J. Raphael-Leff, & R. Jozef Perelberg (Eds.), *Female Experience: Four Generations of British Female Psychoanalysts on their Work with Female Patients,* (pp. 237–257) London: Routledge, 1997; fourth edition, Anna Freud Centre, 2008.

Raphael-Leff, J. (2006). Procreative paradoxes and unconscious representations. In: M. A. Alizade (Ed.), *Motherhood in the 21st Century* (Chapter Thirteen). London: Karnac.

Raphael-Leff, J. (2007). Femininity and its unconscious "shadows": Gender and generative identity in the age of biotechnology. *British Journal of Psychotherapy, 23*: 497–515.

Raphael-Leff, J. (2010a). The gift of gametes: Unconscious motivation and problematics of transcendency. *Feminist Review, 94*: 117–137.

Raphael-Leff, J. (2010b). The "dreamer" by daylight: Imaginative play, creativity and generative identity. *The Psychoanalytic Study of the Child, 64*: 14–53.

Raphael-Leff, J. (2012). The baby-makers: An in-depth single-case study of conscious and unconscious psychological reactions to infertility and "baby-making" technology. In: P. Mariotti (Ed.), *Maternal Lineage* (pp. 205–230). London: Routledge.

Raphael-Leff, J. (2013). Psychic "geodes": The presence of absence. *Couple and Family Psychoanalysis, 3* (In press).

Stoller, R. J. (1985). *Presentations of Gender*. New Haven, CT: Yale University Press.

Tyson, P., & Tyson, R. L. (1990). *Psychoanalytic Theories of Development: An Integration*. New Have, CT: Yale University Press.

Whitman, W. (1855). "Song of Myself". In: *Leaves of Grass* (1818–92). Section 51, The Walt Whitman Archive.

Notes

1. The particular vicissitudes of same-sex couples in becoming parents are beyond the scope of the present paper. In a nutshell, they usually differ in *voluntarily* seeking donated sperm or eggs, a frozen fertilised embryo, or use of a surrogate to achieve their goal of becoming parents.

2. The European Society of Human Reproduction and Embryology ESHRE (2007) cite a wide range, from the highest availability in Israel (3,260 cycles per million population), followed by Denmark, (at 2,031 cycles per million) which also had the greatest proportion of ART births out of all births (3.9%), to Latin American countries (less than 100 cycles per million population) and 0.1% ART births.

3. To accommodate the complexity of contemporary thinking about gender, I have recategorised these components (see Raphael-Leff, 2007). I will not expound on these but focus here on my proposed fourth constituent of *"generative identity"*.

4. Where the child has been conceived through reproductive technology, including IVF, gamete donation, or surrogacy, the situation is complicated by the parents' impotence, needing assistance in procreating a baby, and, in some cases, the child is "haunted" by the unmourned losses of the parents—loss of the wished-for genetically related baby, or of previous miscarriages, stillbirths, or neonatal deaths, especially where these, or the origins of the child, are kept a secret.

5. Italy, Norway, and Germany, for example, ban embryo-freezing, egg donation, and embryo-screening for inherited diseases, forcing couples who need these services to pay for treatment in countries that permit

them, such as Britain, Spain, and Belgium. On the other hand, due to a long waiting list, thousands of British couples who require donated eggs now travel to Spain, Cyprus, and Eastern Europe. Rules on the maximum number of embryos that can be transferred to a woman's womb also differ widely, despite the scientific consensus that the safest policy is to limit implants. In Britain, Scandinavia, and the Low Countries, only one or two embryos may be used, to prevent multiple births—by far the biggest hazard of IVF treatment. Germany and Italy insist that every embryo created is implanted, increasing that risk. Similarly, in the US, where there is no restriction on allocation of sperm, "tribes" of fifty or more half-siblings have found each other through the internet, identified by the donor registration number.

CHAPTER SIX

Overcoming obstacles

Lisa Miller

The foregoing chapters have been about difficulties—serious difficulties—which some parents encounter in the lives of their babies. I should like to put this in perspective by doing two things: by thinking about the ways in which life puts obstacles in the way of everyone, and about how we overcome these obstacles; and also by considering how psychoanalytically informed intervention can help these natural processes to progress and develop. For while it is helpful to think about precise difficulties and the problems they bring, it is also helpful to remember that we can locate them in a wider spectrum, too—the spectrum of experience common to us all. As a young mother who had given birth unexpectedly to a Down syndrome baby said, when confronted by what she felt was too much professional advice: "I thought I'd just like to get to know my baby in the ordinary way first". This chapter is about overcoming obstacles in the ordinary way, remembering that this process is part of everyone's life, that no life is without difficulty and that few are without tragedy.

It is hard to remember that we are born to the human condition. No matter how much we want our babies to be happy and to enjoy life, the fact is that from the beginning life is a mixed affair, and pain is present as much as pleasure. The question for parents, even in the best circumstances, is how to foster in their children delight in good experiences, and also strength to tolerate and live through bad ones. What helps children to develop their capacity to put up with difficulty, to live through it and to learn from the sense of having overcome it? And how does this start from earliest infancy?

First, it may be important to remember that babies and children have a long period of dependency. They don't struggle to their feet and run with the herd like little deer. They need complete looking after for weeks and months, even years, and only gradually as time passes do they become able to look after themselves. This is true not only physically but also mentally. They are not able to comprehend and manage their own experiences for years to come. Infants need the accompaniment of psychologically mature minds to enable them to think about what's happening to them. Two categories of things happen: events take place inside them, both in their bodies and in their minds, and events take place outside them in the dimension of external reality. These two categories, inner and outer, impinge upon each other and influence each other in a constant system of mutual interaction; and the whole experience of getting to know these worlds needs to be presided over by adults who are reasonably benign and stable. A baby is born relationship-seeking, and within the setting of helpful human relations can grow into a person able to develop optimism and perseverance and to tackle obstacles which involve bearing anxiety and trouble.

This is how the ordinary baby grows up. It may help to trace the process back to the moment of birth. Being born is a taxing process in itself, hard work for the mother and hard work for the baby, and some babies need to recoup as from trauma and exhaustion, their powers of endurance already tested. But even for the baby who arrives bright-eyed and calm, a great change has occurred. From being entirely dependent on someone else's system, plugged in to its mother, living her life with her, the infant has to face a challenge. He or she has to make an independent step and take a breath. This is the very first move towards a separate life. But though literally vital for survival, it is only one step. For everything else, the baby is dependent on other people.

The essential bodily needs of this helpless creature are as follows: to be fed, to be cleaned up, and to be protected. There is no way in which a baby can live without someone to feed it, someone to mop up after it, and someone to mind it. This is obvious. Perhaps it is not so obvious that for all three of these basic physical needs there is a psychological concomitant, and that the psychological needs are equally important.

First, there is feeding. Children need good food to grow and to thrive, and also to build up strength and resistance. A malnourished child is vulnerable to infections, illnesses, all the accidents which can happen to a small organism. The baby needs to take in milk which is to be digested and transformed into a strong body. But as good food builds the body, so good experience builds the mind. We can imagine ourselves as having a psychological alimentary canal, a system of the mind which absorbs and assimilates what happens to us and makes us what we are. Too much poor and inadequate food will have a weakening effect, and something similar can happen when the baby's emotional needs are not adequately met. Infants take in more than milk at every feed. They take in affection, they take in the sense of someone who wants to look after them, they take in the idea of a trustworthy person, a person who is interested in them, a person who thinks that they are lovely. One could elaborate this list of good experiences which are absorbed and made part of the child's inner world of memory and imagination, of thought, both conscious and unconscious. These good things are stored away and function as a reserve to draw upon when difficulty, pain, and danger threaten.

There are other ways, too, in which the infant is strengthened. I have said that keeping the baby clean is another vital factor in bodily care, and we know that dirty and unhygienic circumstances carry risks. But the level of care that we take for granted means work—changing nappies, mopping up, bathing, clean clothes. And just as vital is the psychological concomitant. Babies require a great deal of attention to their distress. They are born intelligent but uninformed. The process of learning about the world—both the world out here of other people and outside happenings, and the inner world of their physical and emotional sensations—is one which causes extreme pleasure and extreme pain. Infants easily get panicky and bewildered; they are at the mercy of every bodily twinge and every mental doubt. Their feelings are broadcast immediately in the form of cries for help. They need an adult who can receive these messages and be affected by them—can feel some of the distress and primitive infantile anxiety—but who will not be totally overcome. In fact, a sort of mental soaking-up of distress has to occur.

Babies who sense that their distress is noticed and received feel understood and known. Not all distress can be removed. Neither colicky pains nor panics can always be instantly relieved. But the baby who feels that the adult in charge really takes in some of his or her unhappiness and tries to think what is the matter and to see if it can be made better is a baby who has a chance to take in another kind of good experience—the experience of having someone who sticks to them despite pain and anxiety and doesn't let them down. Sometimes the best we can do for someone else is to keep them company in their distress. The ordinary infant assimilates the idea of someone who does not leave them alone with the problem, but steadfastly puts up with the worry and discomfort involved; this gives the child the opportunity to absorb strength and determination and builds on his or her natural resources and capacity to bear anxiety. Being aware of having faced a difficulty and found this possible is in itself a strengthening experience.

The last physical necessity for an infant is for protection, and this is of various kinds. Keeping a baby safe and warm, holding it when it is upset, defending it from frightening noises and sensations, looking out for dangers—all these are included in the process of looking after somebody who cannot yet look after himself. The overarching function which a parent or carer provides is that of keeping the baby in mind. A new baby needs a person who is preoccupied with him or her, in whose mind he or she lives, someone in a position to give space to the baby in their thoughts; and time, of their adult life, to the child. The absolute need for this diminishes as the baby becomes able to think about him or herself, but as we see from the sad cases of children who have been seriously neglected in inadequate orphanages, the child who has not been thought about cannot learn to think. Multiple indiscriminate caretaking is a disaster. The baby who is not held in mind and remembered is emotionally at risk just as surely as the baby who is not properly cared for in body is at physical risk. A young human being needs at least one person who can bear to have the narrative of the baby's life in their mind, even if the story is a painful one. Babies need, first of all, someone to think for them, then someone to think with them, before they are able to start thinking about themselves.

All this is to demonstrate how babies develop resilience when they grow within the setting of mutual relationships. They bring the capacity for experiencing mutual joy and affection; they bring primitive infantile anxiety stirred up by their vulnerable state. However, parents bring something to the relationship too. They bring their total experience of life to date, everything which has equipped them to be ordinary good parents, and everything which gets in the way of their natural wish to look after their baby well. The previous chapters of this book have been describing situations where there are obvious difficulties, but all babyhoods encounter obstacles to the baby's innate push towards healthy growth and the parents' wish to facilitate this. I shall describe a situation where an observer visiting a family once-weekly saw a situation where difficulties were overcome in an encouraging way over the period of the little boy's first year.

Edmund

Edmund was born following a number of miscarriages, and his early weeks and months were surrounded by an atmosphere of anxiety and discomfort. There had been difficulties in the pregnancy and Edmund was born a little early. Despite this he was a good weight and sucked well; he seemed disposed to tackle life with some optimism. However, by the time he was five weeks old the observer spent an hour with him and his mother which was hardly free at all from miserable unhappy grizzling from the baby, as though he could not make himself comfortable at all. His mother said that he had been like this all week. She walked around cradling him and trying to soothe him, but although Edmund settled briefly as he listened to her voice, it only lasted a short moment before he began another of the intermittent bouts of crying where he scrunched up his whole body, flexed his arms and legs, and belted out his wails. The observer heard a long account of what the mother called constipation in Edmund, but she (the observer) felt a little puzzled, partly because she happened to know that constipation is rare in breast-fed babies, and partly because it did not sound like what she understood as constipation. Edmund's mother said he sometimes only slept for ten minutes after a feed because of this "constipation"; he'd been "a nightmare", she said. However, after nearly an hour, during which the observer felt considerable unease, the baby eventually settled to the breast, and there followed several minutes of blessed silence with both mother and observer becoming entranced by Edmund's rhythmic sucking and his gradual increasingly floppy relaxation.

Here we see a nursing pair who are both anxious. Edmund has a problem in settling in to this world; this made the observer think about the problems the parents had encountered in establishing a pregnancy that would last, one that would bed down and get going. The mother is feeling worried on all three of the fronts I called the basic needs of the baby. The feeding is troubling her—it takes nearly an hour to get Edmund going—and she is bothered because he had latched on so wonderfully well to start with; "he was a natural". Perhaps, she thinks, it's to do with his bottom end and this constipation? She understands the problem in terms of his not being able to deal with states of discomfort. We might think that his distress is hard for her to take in and bear— a problem with the second basic need of mopping up both the dirty nappy and the unhappiness. As for the need for Edmund to be held in mind, there is no doubt but that his mother is totally preoccupied with him, but at the moment he does not seem to be occupying a comfortable place in her mind at all. He's a bit of a nightmare. It looks as though Edmund's discomfort is being added to by his mother's discomfort. In addition to whatever's going on inside him (anxious feelings of not being gathered up and relieved, uncomfortable bodily sensations from his chaotic bowel) the poor boy now has the added problem of a mother who is as worried as he is and perhaps more so. She must be concerned that having at last succeeded in bringing a baby nearly to term and giving birth to a lusty suckling she is somehow going to fail again.

At this time, and for some time after, it is noticeable that Edmund's father never appears when the observer is there. She is perplexed by this, as he is occasionally present in the house but in another room, as was the case in the observation referred to above. Mother feels on her own with the anxiety, which continues to affect the observer. There seems an uncomfortable sense of misunderstanding between mother and baby, with her pulling him off the breast just as he is falling asleep and bouncing him up and down in a jerky way, saying "You love this, don't you?" during an observation a few weeks later. The observer thought the baby wore a look of weary resignation rather than of enjoyment. On another occasion Edmund was rocked quite fast and bumpily in his musical chair, and the observer actually began to feel a bit seasick. At the same time mother was saying that she felt her own confidence had deserted her. She had consulted her health visitor and her doctor.

This ushers in a time when mother is much more tired, less bright and breezy, more half-depressed. Simultaneously, Edmund seems by four and five months old to be more awake, less miserable, only crying when his mother's interest lapses. After a feed, on one occasion, she stands him up on her lap. The observer says he looks "as pleased as Punch", smiling over at her and looking as if he really has taken in something nourishing. Mother is in touch with her own mood, rather exhausted, a bit low, but taking much more interest in what Edmund is actually doing and far less prone to fill the room with anxiety. His development is beginning to reassure her.

Edmund's mother is planning to return to part-time work when the baby is about ten months old. This coincides with a marked shift in the family. In preparation for the change, father plans to work a little less and to share the care of the baby. Father now appears in the observations. The parents give the strong impression of a couple who have found their relationship again. They have discussed plans and worked them out. Reorganisation of the house is taking place, and Edmund has really cheered up. When the observer visits as Edmund turns nine months old, he beams as she enters. Both parents are there; they watch and laugh as Edmund plays dexterously with an old mobile phone. His skills are suddenly developing fast; he plays peekaboo, he swigs from his own bottle of water, he plays a posting game with his mother, and likes to look up at the watching pair—mother and observer—just as he very much likes looking at his mother and father together.

The partnership between the parents is re-established. Obstacles have been overcome as both the nursing couple and the parental couple have linked up. Anxieties which came between them are no longer troubling, and we see, from now on, a much more ordinary course of development, with Edmund particularly relishing his relationship with his father. A space has opened between him and his mother, a distinction has been made between what he is feeling and what she is feeling, and Edmund is much more himself. He recaptures some of the original sturdiness he was said to have been born with.

Pauline

I should like now to turn to a nursing couple who needed help from an external source to overcome the difficulty they were in. Here is a case of a young mother who also brought unsolved problems of her own to the task of bringing up her baby. It is a case I saw many years ago at a GP practice, one which made an impact on me at the time and which taught me some useful things about psychoanalytically oriented interventions with families where the problem appears to be located in the baby, a baby whom I shall call Pauline. The health visitor at the practice asked me to see Pauline and her mother because she was concerned about them: Pauline was having serious problems with sleeping and feeding. She screamed too much, woke repeatedly, and took her bottle in snatches. Her mother was said to be at her wits' end.

I met Pauline and her mother, Mary, and I found a fair, thin, very young woman with a fair, thin baby of about two months. Mary sat with Pauline at a distance from her, facing outwards on her knee. Pauline sat stiffly, all her little fingers rigidly splayed, the very picture of anxiety. In response to my asking, Mary told me that although Pauline had always been rather unsettled, things had got much worse since they had both been ill. She, Mary, had been overtired and picked up some stomach bug which had had a very bad effect, but then Pauline had got it. Pauline had become seriously dehydrated with diarrhoea and vomiting, and she had been admitted to hospital. Her mother was persuaded not to go into hospital with her but to stay at home and recover herself. Pauline had come back cured but desperate. She refused to be comforted by her mother, she turned away from the bottle, she cried and could not sleep properly. Naturally she lost weight. Her mother became frantic with worry.

As the conversation continued, Mary volunteered more about her own life. She told me that her own mother had died when she, Mary, was eleven. Nevertheless, she had managed her schooling and was proud of having had a job at a well-known department store. She was married; she married at eighteen a young man of twenty who had been her boyfriend at school, and they had Pauline within the year. I had the impression that her husband simply did not know what had hit him. His parents were doing their best, but the extreme nature of Mary and Pauline's distress frightened them. On both sides the couple came from big families which were in one way warm and united; but they descended from generations where poverty and large numbers of children meant that individuals probably received little attention.

Mary's story evoked considerable anxiety in me. Equally anxiety-provoking was Pauline's half-starved appearance; they looked like my idea of a nineteenth-century workhouse pair, and yet I knew that there was no material lack—the young father had a very reasonable job. I suggested meeting again in a week's time. My anxiety was redoubled when a week later Mary told me that Pauline had slept less than ever and eaten less. She continued in this vein, and I felt I could discern a fury in her voice. I listened and eventually suggested that it must be quite upsetting, even annoying, when Pauline kept on saying no to the bottle. All at once Mary spilled out how bad she felt that she hadn't tried harder to breast-feed, how she'd been breast-fed herself; and then how angry she was with Pauline, how fed up she was with all of this, how she wished she hadn't got married; and then how dreadful she felt to be so furious with her own baby. Sometimes she hated Pauline. She wept.

I myself was filled with renewed anxiety. The session time had ended, and I did not know what to do. The only more encouraging sign was that, as Mary's tirade ended, Pauline and I looked at each other. Pauline leant towards me and gave a lovely smile. I instantly thought that Mary might feel envious—why should this stranger get acknowledgement? But no; Mary looked at me too. "She likes you", she said in quite a warm tone. I spent a worried week. I rang the health visitor, saying I was still concerned and urging her to visit. I awaited the next appointment with apprehension.

However, Mary presented with Pauline in a different mood. Pauline really had been eating and sleeping better; she had put on some weight. We talked about more general matters of managing a baby, and Mary asked if her husband could come next time. Indeed, he did come, and an optimistic atmosphere prevailed. I heard the story of a family christening where Pauline had been smiley and much admired—indeed, it was another baby who had cried. With this the family passed out of my acquaintance, and I am left thinking that Pauline must be of an age to have her own children by now. One can see how deprivation and loss can be passed down the years and wonder to what extent Mary's bereavement, against a background of generations of impoverishment, will have shown through in the next generation.

I said that I thought I had learnt from this case, and the question now is if we can learn something about overcoming obstacles with the help of a brief intervention from outside. What exactly was the obstacle in question? First of all, Pauline was being deprived of what she needed. Something had disturbed her to the point where she could not take in what her mother wanted to give. It looked as if this had been going on to some extent even before the pair were taken ill. We may speculate that Mary had a specific difficulty in becoming a mother which was connected to her bereavement. Certainly she spoke of her mother's death early on in the first meeting as though she was aware that it was important. It is a serious lack when a teenage girl does not have a mother in vigorous middle age, able to deal with some of the conflicts and stresses aroused by adolescent development. Instead, Mary had a gap where that mother should have been; perhaps also a gap in her own process of maturing which she bridged by latching on to a boyfriend at school and hurrying into motherhood. It was as though Mary felt, as a smaller girl can do with a doll, that you can grow up by magic and be a mummy if you have a baby. Pauline was of course not a doll but a living human being with emotions and anxieties all her own to contribute to the relationship. Most, perhaps all, first-time mothers struggle with the feeling that they can't manage at times—the unconscious feeling that they are elder sisters left in sole full-time charge of the baby, rather than grown women assuming with some effort the task of becoming a mother. What sustains them in the ordinary way is not only the actual support of partner or grandmother but also the inner and unconscious sense that the mother of their imagination is helping them. Mary was feeling totally let down, as though her mother had deserted her.

It became clear how angry she felt, and how Pauline seemed a living reproach. Every time Pauline refused her bottle or cried inconsolably it was as though she were saying to her mother, "You aren't a proper mother, you can't breast-feed, you're just a child pretending". Mary felt Pauline despised her. When things broke down and they both became ill with persecutory pains and vomitings it seemed to mother and baby, we may imagine, as though their worst fears had been realised—all goodness gone, a sense that must have been increased for Pauline by the loss of her mother when she was admitted to hospital.

What was it that enabled them to recoup? There is no doubt but that both of them did have resources, just as Mary did actually have a husband and a mother-in-law who were concerned. In a psychoanalytically based intervention we value the power of the transference and have faith, based on experience, in change taking place as a result of something actually happening in the room. In this intervention a relationship, operating on an unconscious level, sprang up unbidden. Mary felt that I had understood the seriousness of her anxieties. This is partly confirmed by the strength of the anxiety I took away and carried around. I was really worried about her. One could say that Mary felt looked after, as though her internal mother woke up and started to take notice. She felt that she was in the presence of someone who would do her best not only to look after her, but also to look after her baby; someone who could think about two people at once. This was confirmed when she noticed that Pauline smiled at me and was pleased. It made Mary feel as though Pauline wasn't so damaged after all, just as she felt that she wasn't such an awful person, as she had feared, since I hadn't reacted with horror to what she told me.

Consequently, Mary was better able to take sympathy and help from her husband, who himself started to feel less useless and more manly. Both, together, looked after Pauline, who (like Edmund) cheered up when she felt that the fundamental relationships—between mother and baby and between a parental couple—were being repaired and when her mother became more able to keep an adult perspective, feeding and caring for her in a less anxious and agitated way.

The meaning of the baby

Each baby carries its own meaning for the parents who made it, just as all parents carry a charge of significance for their children which extends far beyond their individual personalities and acts. In psychoanalytic terms the oedipal cluster of thoughts, emotions, and phantasies or unconscious imaginings are central to the unfolding of our characters. The questions "Who made me?" and "Who brought me up?" are universal. In our unconscious minds the figures of mother, father, and siblings are present for ever: not as direct representations of the actual people in our families, but as something more complex. We do not have to have had brothers and sisters for our deep ideas about sibs to form and colour our relations with peers in the place we learn or work or live; and in our minds the figures of mother and father continue to influence us because they are indissolubly part of our world. A parental couple bring their concepts of what it means to be a father and a mother, and what it means to have a baby, to the creative act and the business of bringing up children.

In ordinary good circumstances having a baby is felt to be a hopeful thing, an optimistic step into the future. Parents are unconsciously identified with the creative mother and father of their imaginings, who are felt to be benign and encouraging to the new generation. However, these figures of the imagination do not have to be good; we are all still children at some level, prone to fearing witches and giants and bad gods who are against us, not for us. New babies stir us deeply, and when things go wrong we do not only respond as rational adults.

In both the examples just quoted the parents' faith, in becoming good parents who are supported from within by their own helpful mothers and fathers, was shaken. Edmund's parents were shaken by the experience of repeated miscarriages, and they felt as though they must be getting something terribly wrong to be punished by failure time and again. It took them months to re-establish the idea of a couple who could get things right. For them, and also for Pauline's parents, the presence of a scared and jittery baby challenged their belief in their power to grow into parenthood. It seems as though the gods were against them. However, in both cases these were people who had had sufficient good experiences—no doubt starting in their own infancies—to be able to recapture the identification with kind, capable parents.

Complications associated with conception, pregnancy, or birth challenge a couple's inner resources and alter the meaning of having a baby. When everything is straightforward and a healthy baby is born to a couple who are united in their welcome and determined upon a joint enterprise, it is obvious that the weather is set fair: the natural ups and down of babyhood are likely to prove temporary and surmountable obstacles. In many cases where there are problems the eventual presence of a live baby overrides previous dread. But in some cases the facts surrounding a child's conception have a tendency to overshadow the child's early life.

For instance, twins were born to a couple whose previous little baby had died. These twins were a boy and a girl. The dead baby had been a girl. All through the twins' early life the mother was aware that while the boy prospered, the girl seemed discontented, difficult, mutinous. The father was less worried. It was as though the boy was free to live his own life, as though the sun were shining on him more than on his sister. It became clear that the girl meant something very different from the boy, especially to the mother. The child felt like a reproach to her mother, as Pauline had to hers. First, the unhappy ghost of the dead baby hung around her. The mother had been even more deeply affected than one might think and felt as though she had been robbed. This second girl seemed to look at her with an air of dislike and distrust. Difficulties multiplied, and perhaps were even increased by everyone's natural tendency to compare siblings; in this case of twins, one as easy and one as a problem. This girl was seen through a multiplicity of lenses which prevented her mother from seeing her as a straightforwardly good baby who loved her. However, the balanced state of mind of the father was a saving grace, and the parents sought some counselling—a regular time set aside to think together about the meaning of this unhappy situation.

From the point of view of overcoming obstacles, a complex situation like this needs much thought and attention over the years. Adult co-operation, perseverance, and the determination never to give up meant that matters never deteriorated as they might have done and gradually the problems faded. The once acute difference perceived between the twins was replaced by a more steady view that each was an individual with a separate disposition.

Babies who bring their own difficulties

So far we have considered only babies who are fundamentally well. Clearly, if a baby is premature or ill there are serious obstacles to the ordinary processes of emotional development. Feeding, making a baby comfortable, keeping it company, are all desperately painful tasks for both child and parent when the child is labouring under this kind of disadvantage. Putting up with unbearable primitive anxiety is the task which Maggie Cohen writes about in her chapter. My argument has been that although the levels of pain are extreme when circumstances are extreme, the process of absorbing and acknowledging pain is the same in ordinary infancy, and that the struggle to keep paying attention is central.

David

Prematurity is a disadvantage whose effects can be mitigated. I remember years ago when I was working in brief counselling with parents and their under-fives, a mother came to talk about her two-year-old son, David. It became clear that she had two years' worth of things to tell me, a whole unprocessed narrative which needed attention and sorting out. David had been premature and had been in hospital for a long time. His mother, Helen, let the whole story of his unexpected premature birth tumble out. It seemed to have happened yesterday. But a factor she stressed again and again was how she had thrown herself into the care of the tiny infant. She stayed in hospital and earned respect from the nursing staff. She was just as good as a nurse, somebody said. It was as if Helen clung to this suggestion and identified herself with her over-idealised idea of a perfect nurse—someone always calm and capable, someone who never panicked and always knew what to do. Any real nurse could say that this is not what a nurse feels like, but Helen was out of touch with the reality of what was going on around her, and out of touch with her own feelings, let alone the truth of David's feelings.

However, from the time when she took her baby home she felt overwhelmed by the vulnerability of this tiny person. She told of what a struggle the last two years had been. When I met him I met a toddler who embodied the phrase "all over the place". He could hardly settle to anything. He up-ended a box of small toys, he clambered on the furniture, he tried to get into my desk drawers and my handbag. David could not sit peacefully for a minute and he could not play. His mother asked tentatively whether I thought he had ADHD. I thought there were other ways of understanding what the matter was.

To begin with, as I have already said, the narrative of David's life was far from clear in his mother's mind. The story was infused with anxiety and his mother's sense of guilt and resentment. What had gone wrong? Helen had been unable to think over the events of his life. Certainly, she had been able to brood upon them—but not to think about them in a way which enabled her to make some sense of them and get on with the job of bringing him up. She was still regarding him with immense anxiety. As she watched him climbing about she said, several times, that she didn't know what to do with him—he wouldn't stop. David was being given the experience of being unmanageable. His mother was depressed and agitated.

Subsequent conversations showed how Helen found it hard to help David with becoming able to think about how he was feeling. She had originally found it too excruciating to bear witness to his distress and to acknowledge her worry about his survival. This situation was continuing. She could not see how his jumpy, unhappy behaviour, veering between clinginess and outbursts, was a manifestation of baby anxiety. Instead, she was frightened that something was deeply wrong with him. The medical staff had always been reassuring about David's development, but she was convinced that they were mistaken. David, of course, was indeed conveying that something was wrong—but it was not simply physical.

It is common for children, particularly little boys, to become overanxious and over-active when their mothers are depressed, whether or not prematurity is an issue. They feel their mother is unreachable, that their messages are unheard, and their attempts to rouse her get increasingly desperate. Their wish to bring a smile to her face is unfulfilled. For David, this had started very early. His mother had taken refuge in efficient and busy caring activities, but was mentally out of touch with the baby trying to reach her. Now she needed help to think about his current unmanageable anxiety, the direct descendent of his earliest states, as well as to think retrospectively about their time in hospital which haunted the family like unfinished business.

Kaya

Here is an example of another baby, Kaya, who is causing anxiety because she has been born with a slight internal abnormality which will need surgical intervention. We see parents who are not quite in touch with how worried they are, and a baby who is restless and anxious.

At this point in the observations Kaya is six months old. Her operation is imminent. Her parents have been reassured that a favourable outcome is likely (and so it proved to be) but beneath the surface all is anxiety. The family consists of Kaya's mother, Ann, her father, Derek, and her much older sister, Tara. Ann is usually very chatty and cheerful, even over-bright. But today she is obviously finding things too much. She and Kaya have spent the day at grandma's house.

The observer comes in to the living-room where the television is loudly playing. Kaya sits with her back to it and mother is feeding her on rather surprisingly lumpy food. "I'm trying to get her to chew", she says. "Mmmmm, you need to chew", she tells Kaya as the baby appears undecided, wrinkles her nose and lets a large lump fall out of her mouth. Kaya turns her gaze to the observer. Ann offers another spoonful. "Chew!" Rather than chatting away as usual Ann focuses her attention fixedly on Kaya. "This bowl seems never-ending", she says. Kaya continues to gaze at the observer as she plays with the food with her tongue. "That's it, chew, good girl!" Kaya remains fixated on the observer. "Don't stare, it's rude", Ann says, but Kaya ignores her. Mother speaks to the baby in an increasingly high-pitched voice, and rather insistently.

Derek comes home. He says hello to everyone and "Hiya!" to Kaya who returns a welcoming smile. Ann continues to feed her. Derek goes out but soon comes back to sit down. "How's she been?" he asks. Ann explains at length that as soon as she got home from her mum's Kaya started to cry continuously. Ann thought it was her teeth and gave her teething gel, but in the end she calmed down a bit. She says it was "weird", because the baby was fine at her grandma's but as soon as she got back home she began to cry and wouldn't stop. "I had to get Tara just to sit with her for five minutes—I needed time out, it was so constant". Derek nods. "This bowl is never-ending", says Ann again. "If it was pudding you'd have eaten it", she tells Kaya. Kaya coughs. She seems to be choking. She swallows. Tears form in her eyes. "Chew, chew, choo like a train", says her mum.

The meal continues, and Kelly does get some custard which she eats more easily. At the end the exhausted Ann asks Derek to sit with Kaya while she goes outside for a cigarette. Her father plays lively games, clapping, snapping his fingers, bouncing her, but half-watching the television himself. The observer worries inwardly that the baby might be sick—she ate a big meal and is now being tossed about. This doesn't happen but just before the end of the observation Kaya throws herself backwards in a violent arching movement on dad's lap and gives three loud, disturbing, high-pitched screams.

At this point in time Kaya is being asked to bear extra anxiety, the anxiety which her parents can't quite cope with and absorb. Kaya is thrown back on the reserves of good experiences which she undoubtedly has had, but which are under pressure. There is a background of the bright and over-jolly approach which in this family is associated with trying to cheer themselves up. It masks or even denies worry. This is in evidence from the start with the loud unwatched television filling in the background silence. Against this background Ann is making Kaya take in food she doesn't like. The food is lumpier than anything the observer has seen Kaya have before; it is unwelcome, but Kaya is making an effort to comply. It suggests that Ann herself is burdened with unwelcome anxiety. This must surely be linked with anxiety about the baby's physical state and her forthcoming operation, thoughts which the mother finds it hard to assimilate and digest. She seems to be feeding Kaya with anxiety, spooning it in with the hard lumps.

It sounds as though they were both more or less all right while they were at grandma's house and grandma was there to look after her daughter a little, but once the two of them were home again Kaya sensed her mother's anxiety and broke into sobs which could hardly be comforted. Ann for her part admits that she found it too hard to bear the sobs and had to have "time out", as if the idea of her baby suffering was too much for her.

Kaya gets full up with all the lumpy stuff, both literally and metaphorically, and chokes on it. At the end of the meal mum is full up too and has to go outside. Dad resorts to his joking and bouncing the baby, as if to throw out the anxiety, and doesn't really concentrate upon her. The observer fears it may cause Kaya to throw up, as though the whole experience were too much to take in, and at the end Kaya gives disturbing shrieks. The observer feels these to be anguished. Dad ignores them and watches the TV.

What we see here is a baby being brought up in an everyday family by ordinary good parents. But what we also see is how hard they are finding it to confront the idea that Kaya may have an unpleasant experience in store in hospital. Even more difficult are all the associated ideas about her vulnerability which must be present, at least unconsciously. No matter how rationally they seek reassurance, Kaya's parents, like all parents of a child who needs hospital care, are brought up against the fact that we cannot protect our children from everything, and we cannot even keep them alive simply by willing it. Ann is expressing the fact that fate is forcing an unwanted experience on her baby and herself, and Derek too is expressing, in his lack of attention, how helpless he feels. The overall effect is to leave Kaya alone with the worries which they convey to her.

What a relief for the whole family when Kaya's operation was successfully carried out and when they could return to a state where their trust in a reasonable degree of good fortune was restored. It seemed as though Kaya's parents' trust in their power to look after their baby was challenged, as was inevitable, but the result was to pass on to Kaya anxieties which they could not deal with themselves—at least at this particular moment in time.

Conclusion

The main theme of this chapter—overcoming obstacles—has been to consider the basic ways in which a child is helped to develop resilience in the face of difficulties, with some thought about the challenges that face parents in painful circumstances. But although all the families that have been described here were facing some degree of unusual difficulty in their children's lives, the process which takes place to try to overcome the difficulties is the same process that takes place constantly in the bringing up of any child.

A child is dependent on the help of a more grown-up person whose reserves of psychological strength and of life experience are greater. But help does not always mean removing the difficulty. In some situations that would be undesirable. For instance, if a child is having difficulty in learning to read, the solution is not to take away the book; indeed, the more this is done, the more the child will feel the adult agrees that reading is too hard for him or her. The solution is far more likely to lie in acknowledging that there is a difficulty but sticking it out and persevering, despite all the unpleasant emotions that trying to read are arousing. This is true even in grave circumstances where a straightforward solution is impossible. Every anxiety faced, every difficulty worked through rather than evaded, brings a growth in emotional muscle. The more that an infant or a child has close contact with adults who can bear this process, the better. Then there is a chance to develop increasing strength, and the growing capacity to deal independently with obstacles that lie in life's way.

INDEX